SHEENA TA

Perfectly
Imperfect
Mum

The Book Guild Ltd

First published in Great Britain in 2020 by
The Book Guild Ltd
9 Priory Business Park
Wistow Road, Kibworth
Leicestershire, LE8 0RX
Freephone: 0800 999 2982
www.bookguild.co.uk
Email: info@bookguild.co.uk
Twitter: @bookguild

Typeset in 10pt Avenir

Printed and bound by CPI Group (UK) Ltd, Croydon, CR0 4YY

ISBN 978 1913208 929

British Library Cataloguing in Publication Data.
A catalogue record for this book is available from the British Library.

My husband Piyus for endless patience and kindness
My daughters Sienna and Isla for endless inspiration and cuddles

Contents

Who Am I

Hi, I would love to introduce myself to you all!

I am a perfectly imperfect mum of two beautiful little beings aged eight and six. This part of the journey alone has taught me to be strong, resilient and patient, but also to be kind, not just to my children but also to myself.

I am also an optometrist, rapid transformation therapy and NLP practitioner, life coach, mindfulness and meditation practitioner, and also a vegetarian and vegan nutritionist.

I have faced many challenges pre and during motherhood, including stress, anxiety and being overwhelmed. For a huge part of my life, these emotions controlled me, I couldn't seem to find a way out and I would usually end up on the floor with tears rolling down my face, not really sure how I could face another day. I also knew I couldn't carry on like this. I needed to be there for my girls; I was their comfort and security and needed to be strong to be able to do this. I needed to take control of my life and master my thoughts, not let my thoughts master me.

As much as wanting to inspire my girls was a driving force, I also needed to change for me too. I needed to start living, feel happier, maintain it in the best way possible and embrace being perfectly imperfect.

Over time and through various methods of studying and self-learning, I feel like I have finally found the core methods that have had a positive, huge impact and shift on me and my family. I went from stressed, overwhelmed and anxious on a daily basis to running two businesses (Inspiring Success and Pure and Raw Goodies) and loving being a mum. I am able to use simple yet effective techniques in everyday life to ensure we have a positive experience as a family. Of course we can still have our crazy chaotic moments, but it's all about managing them and not letting them take over. I am super excited to share this with you and support you in your beautiful journey of motherhood.

Connect with me at:

- www.inspiring-success.com
- Facebook: sheenasinspiringsuccess
- Instagram: @sheenasinspiringsuccess
  @pureandrawgoodiessheena

Introduction

So you are a wondering if this book is for you, am I right? Well, let me help you decide with the following questions:

- *Are you a mum or responsible for younger dependents?*
- *Is life chaotic, with the never-ending kids' to-do list?*
- *Can some weeks seem overwhelming?*
- *Are you trying to find your own identity amongst the mum madness?*
- *Are you trying to live (and survive) a perfect life in an imperfect world? (Did you have to think about that one?)*

If the answer is YES to even one of those questions, then this book is for you.

This book has been created with YOU in mind, the person who is juggling all the different-sized plates on one leg without falling to keep the show going.

Every mum has their own story and own journey, but one thing that we have in common is the love we have for our kids and how we would do anything for them and their happiness. However, through the endless dinners, laundries, taxi runs, clubs and constantly wondering if we are getting it right, we can often lose our grip at times. Often when we do lose the plot, and maybe get a little hysterical, we don't know where to turn. Now take a moment to imagine this: you wake up, it's beautifully silent, the kids are dressed and doing homework, one even brings you a frothy coffee with chocolate sprinkles and asks what you'd like for breakfast, and even if there's any snacks they could bring up. You happily laze around the whole day with no disturbance whilst the kids make all the meals and decline needing any form of entertainment or even leaving the house. Pure bliss.

Now I can't guarantee you that level of bliss; however I can definitely give you fantastic ways to feel the calm in the chaos, embrace the challenging days, love the connection you can have with the kids, all whilst keeping you sane and giving you the self-care that you truly deserve.

This book is structured with various scenarios that us mums will encounter at some point during the week or month. It's these typical scenarios where having one too many of them can often lead us to a meltdown. The aim is that when you are going through a certain scenario you can now change your whole perspective on it and how you approach it from beginning to end.

Each scenario will have a mindfulness and motivational tip to really allow you to reframe your mindset so you have a more positive experience. It could be about positive self-dialogue, the way you view a situation, the connection you have with your child during this time, and how to really be mindful and live in the moment instead of thinking about the next item on the to-do list. The tasks and jobs will remain the same, but how you view and take them on can be changed. This part will show you how to fully embrace the situation and be present.

Each scenario will have a mouth-watering, delicious and yet very nutritious simple go-to recipe. This recipe has been created to perfectly complement that particular scenario. The go-to recipe will be bursting with nourishing nutrients, and even if you aren't a baker or creator, these are designed to be very simple yet effective so anyone can have a go. You can try it alone or have some fun in the kitchen and get the kids involved too.

Each scenario will also have a complementary yoga pose or movement. The purpose of having the yoga pose or movement is to really help you connect with your body which is constantly on the move. Whether it allows a stretch, deep relaxation or simple connection, it will serve a form of benefit. Our thoughts and emotional feelings will always have a physical reaction, so having the body move to alleviate any of these tensions and stresses will help.

All movements and poses are suitable to all levels, but of course always check with a GP if you are unsure about anything. These poses are also suitable for the kids to join in too.

Connecting the mind (mindfulness and motivation) and body (yoga and food) will allow you to feel whole and complete and be able to take on any day full of energy. You can take on all segments of the scenario, or simply pick the one that you are drawn to. You can go through all the chapters or simply go to the one you may be experiencing that day. There is no right or wrong way to use the book; the perfect way to use the book is to use it imperfectly. Read it back to front, bottom to top, start from the middle; your way is the only way.

I have added extra tools and tips at the back for you to use as and when you wish. This book is designed for all you mums to thrive and not just survive the day, week or year. Live for each moment and milestone, and enjoy the journey of motherhood but also connecting to you too.

Three Concepts of the Book

Mindful Parent

What is mindfulness and why do I need it? (PS, I need a good reason as to why extra chocolate can't be the answer for everything.)

Mindfulness plays a vital role in allowing us to be aware of, manage, and control our thoughts and emotions. Thoughts really can run away from us and spiral very quickly, causing us to lose control of all actions and behaviours that follow. If you imagine a dog that hasn't been well trained, you will feel like the dog is controlling you; you'd be running after it, feeling exhausted and not really knowing what it's going to do next. If you imagine the same dog trained, you would actually enjoy its company and spending time with it. The same is for you when your thoughts are all over the place, running from one thing to another and not knowing how to manage it all. Being mindful allows you to control these thoughts, giving you better focus, clarity and energy to know what to do next and how to respond.

Often we are living in the past (regret mode) or future (worry mode) and as a result are missing out on the gift which is the present. We are also trying to multi-task so our attention is spread over different things and therefore never giving one hundred per cent to one thing.

We use the words 'time flies', or 'look how big they are getting' or 'how old they are' when referring to the kids, but if we practise mindfulness we can always be assured that we enjoy every minute with them and the experience as a mum at each stage.

Children are very often naturally mindful; my daughter, for example, when she reads a book will have to really focus on the words a few times to build a picture in her mind – she wants to be in the scene of her story. If there are pictures, she wants to know which picture is the right character so she can really feel the story. Yes, this all may take a little longer at bedtime, but so what? I don't want her losing her ability to be mindful. When she's talking excitedly about something, she's feeling every emotion in her body; nothing about yesterday or tomorrow, she's living in the moment, and it's beautiful to see.

Practising mindfulness reduces stress and anxiety, and improves mood, confidence, social interactions, self-awareness and can even help physical health issues such as lowering blood pressure.

Nourished Mum

Food and drink can really have a huge impact on your mood and energy. I completely revamped my nutrition after my second child, as I realised biscuits were not sustainable fuel for energy. I also wanted to be enjoying my kids and not think about my next sugar fix, and I wanted my family to be a part of the healthy changes so that they could be fully boosted internally too.

Small changes can really start leading to it being part of everyday life. A good, balanced diet is key for a good, balanced mood. Allowing your blood sugar levels to remain stable allows your frame of mind to be stable; it can keep your energy, and therefore your mood, stable throughout the day. When you eat the 'comfort foods', such as quite sugary or starchy foods, they may give you the 'feel-good factor', but only for a short period. They trigger the happy centres in the brain due to increased blood sugar but will give you a crash later on.

Some food can stimulate production of certain brain chemicals which manage many things, including your emotions. One of these chemicals is dopamine, which is responsible for concentration, being alert and feeling good. Foods to boost dopamine include protein-rich food like tofu, lentils, beans and milk.

Another chemical is serotonin; this is responsible for managing sleep, anxiety and mood. Foods to boost this include cacao, oats, quinoa and seeds.

Endorphin is another chemical that helps promote feelings of joy and gives you a boost of happiness. When released into the bloodstream they give a feeling of euphoria and reduce feelings of pain and stress. Foods to help this include strawberries, grapes, nuts, seeds, cacao and ginseng.

Oxytocin helps with relaxation and is also known as the 'love hormone', building stronger relationships and boosting empathy and care. Food to help this include bananas, avocados, spinach, watermelon, legumes, nuts and seeds.

Yogi Mum

Yoga has many physical and mental health benefits. Yoga means union, and this is the union of the mind and body. Emotions can often trigger physical health issues in the body;

yoga can help ease this physical discomfort. It will also improve flexibility, strength and posture; all things which need to be taken care of when you are taking care of kids.

The psychological impact yoga has shown to have includes increased emotional stability, being more in tune with the mind and body, improved quality of sleep, a positive frame of mind, and improved concentration and clarity, to name a few. In this book we look at various postures (asanas). How you hold your body will influence how you feel; if you walk around slumped with a lowered head you probably won't feel great, but if you stand tall and in control you will begin to feel that. Yoga postures balance and strengthen the internal network of the whole body, including the nervous systems and endocrine system. They also release any tension in the muscle built up from emotional stress.

When you are caring for others in the best way possible, it is essential you care for yourself in exactly the same way. Looking after yourself from the inside – mind, body and soul – will allow you to deal with any and every external circumstance in the best way.

ONE

Secret Mum

OK, let's be honest, how many of you have a secret separate stash of chocolate just for YOU? The one you secretly snack on when the kids are occupied elsewhere, the little nibble here or there that you savour, and a moment you look forward to as you bustle the kids out of the kitchen. The rest of the family have no idea of your secret storage; they assume there is only one treat or snack cupboard/ drawer that is available for the whole family.

How many of you are pouring gin into your thermoses or water bottle as you get ready to take the kids to their activity? The kids mistakenly take your extra cheering as enthusiasm rather than being slightly tipsy. Or the time when your child comes down after supposedly being in bed for a few hours to find you sprawled on the sofa with a glass of red? You tell them you have literally been squeezing berries for a nourishing hydrating boost. Or when they unexpectedly make an appearance and you, quick as a flash, crumple any wrappers and wipe your face?

(I remember eating my daughter's party bag cake after she forgot about it. I hid it quickly behind the curtain after eating it and forgot about it; a day later she discovered it and was not impressed!)

Have you been saving up all your F words to have the biggest offload as soon as your partner comes home or get on the phone to the nearest person that will listen? Telling your children all day about being polite, having manners, not to yell or be rude. Now here you are, f-ing and blinding and sounding like the most unmumsy mum. What is it about swearing that somehow makes you feel better?

Maybe you have had a day off or work from home. Instead of doing the to-do list (or telling yourself you'll do it in half an hour), you've had a little mooch to the shops, popped out for lunch, had a few extra cups of teas and, during whatever time was left, had a Netflix binge. When you've been questioned about what you have been up to all day, you roll your eyes and explain it's been a chaotic day catching up with the tidying, online food shop, kids' appointments and how time just ran away. You also throw in the fact you've only drank tea and not even had time to eat lunch or think about food – maybe a takeaway would be easier, just for today?

The guilty-pleasure moments, the stolen precious few minutes, the secret binge days, the secret drinking and swearing mummy that we have found ourselves getting morphed into is almost quite comical when looking from the outside. However, they can turn into addictions and also often start causing segregation within the family. When we feel we need these moments to feel better or survive, we can tend to look forward to them more than time spent within the family. Yes, some moments are definitely needed for you, but always ensure there is a balance.

Mindfulness and Motivation Tips

Mindful eating

Be mindful when eating at family times – really immerse yourself in the food and enjoy the whole experience together. Instead of doing jobs whilst the kids eat, or letting the kids watch TV during mealtimes, aim to sit and eat as a family. Practising mindful eating will allow you to feel fuller and more satisfied. You wouldn't even need the treat for the feel-good factor.

Treats

If you do have a treat, have it as a family. It doesn't need to be seen as something bad and something to be denied or only eaten as a reward. See it as enjoying something together, knowing as a family that even though there may be no nutritional benefits, it's OK to enjoy it in moderation. Often when treats are viewed as to be had only at certain times, this can lead to addictions later on. Treats are often viewed as only being consumed during good times (maybe in your own childhood you were only given treats when you did something good or it was a special occasion) so often as adults, to conjure the same feel good feeling, the same treats are eaten in excess. Also if you do want to eat a biscuit or chocolate, don't always feel you need to hide it; when I choose to have something I now have it in front of the kids if they have happen to be there instead of waiting for them to be out of sight. They know that healthy eating is important to me and know that if I want to indulge now and then, then that too is OK. (Oh, sometimes I may give in and share, and sometimes I really won't.)

Moments for yourself are precious, so make them count

Take a moment to think before you react or reach for the wine. Does my action really have a purpose; could I do something else for the same effect? Could you instead have a bath, read a book, contact a friend or arrange a date? Be mindful of your thoughts, observe and then take action. Is it more beneficial to wake up with a hangover and face another school day, or wake up fully rested after a nice long bath? If you still want a glass, that's absolutely OK, but just take that moment to check in with yourself and ask why.

When you have a day off, ENJOY IT

You don't have to feel guilty for taking time out. Just like the ironing can pile up on the ironing board, so can the stresses on your mind. To iron the stresses out, you need time to be YOU and not playing the role of mum, daughter, partner or colleague. You are entitled to days off without justifying it, so absolutely enjoy it. Do whatever it is that makes you relax. Be OK with it, but also be honest with it. When the kids come home, be open and say you had some time for yourself and the fun you had; this shows them that you're your own person too and not just the cook, cleaner and chauffeur.

Nourish

Turmeric Milk Latte/
Cacao Hot Chocolate

I love nothing more than wrapping my hands around a warm mug filled with a nourishing hot drink. I absolutely love milk lattes, and more often than not they have no coffee. You may be thinking, what? Trust me, the nurturing and nourishing ingredients won't leave you longing for caffeine.

Recipe

Ingredients

- 1 cup/mug milk of your choice
- ½ teaspoon turmeric or heaped tablespoon cacao (you can also try matcha tea or blue spirulina; I love the beautiful colours these ingredients create)
- 1 teaspoon of coconut sugar or agave

Method

1. Heat a mug of milk of your choice (I love almond milk) either in a pan, frother or steamer.
2. Add the turmeric or the cacao powder.
3. Add the sweetener (extra if desired).
4. Optional to add a pinch of cinnamon, cardamom or allspice.
5. Mix together and enjoy.

Yoga Pose

Superwoman Pose

Embrace the superwoman mum that you are. Show the world you really are a hero and not afraid to show or celebrate it.

Direction

1. Lay on the floor, flat on your belly.
2. Reach your arms out to the side with palms flat on the floor and facing down.
3. Bring your legs together and give yourself a good stretch.
4. Inhale and lift as much of your body off the mat as you can, hold for a breath and release back on the mat. Repeat two more times.

Benefits

- Stretches and strengthens your chest, arms, legs and glutes.
- Improves your circulation and energises you.

TWO

Judged Mum

———————————

Wow! Where to even begin with this one! Prior to having my own kids I would be the one secretly judging other parents on their parenting skills – you know, the typical, "If that was my child, I would never give them choice at mealtimes, they would eat what I make or go hungry," "I will never go for rides in the car in an attempt to get my child to fall asleep," "I would never give them biscuits as a snack; it will always be fruit or vegetables," "My kids would never throw a tantrum like that," etc., etc. Then I had my own children – OH MY GOD, not only was I judging my own choices, I felt I was being judged by my family, schoolteachers, passengers on the plane, waitresses, passers-by, shoppers and, of course, OTHER MUMS!

The minute a friend was due over, the TV would be switched off and educational games placed on the floor, often arranged like we'd been playing for hours. When out with the family, there would be vegetable sticks and hummus for snacks, and I would pretend it was hilarious when the kids told me they thought I'd mistakenly bought cucumber fingers instead of chocolate fingers.

Just when you think you have survived one phase of parenthood and you are feeling smug, the next phase hits you and you are back to searching for the parenting manual. Whether it's your mum telling you that back in her day everything was much simpler and maybe you should try this that and the other as it worked for her, and if not then a couple of extra biscuits will fix everything (being Indian, that usually meant six biscuits). Whether it's looking at other mums across the playground, elegantly dressed, make-up on, packed lunch and homework at the ready, chirpy and engaging, all at 8.30am in the morning (whilst you have just managed to brush you hair... or did you forget that morning?). If it's the neighbours giving you the death stare as you drive out because things were a little on the loud and lively side during the bedtime routine, or you are on the plane and your child has been on the iPad for over an hour whilst the random kid in the opposite aisle has been quietly reading a book eating an apple.

We want to be the fun mum, strict mum, cool mum, got-her-****-together mum, stylish mum, PTA mum, work mum, mumsy mum, on-time mum, but playing all these roles and ALL AT THE SAME TIME is pretty exhausting! With this mental exhaustion, all we will then focus on is seeing these traits in other mums.

Our minds for sure can exaggerate what we see and perceive, but when we are feeling fragile as parents it's easy to assume we are being judged and if not by others, definitely by ourselves. The time had come for me to be the most unique, one-of-a-kind mum there could possibly be... by being simply ME, and if you are experiencing any of the above then it's absolutely time for you to feel good being YOU.

Celebrate being one-of-a-kind

One vital thing to remember in this present moment is there is no mum in the entire world like you; you are incredibly unique and that makes you very special. That also makes your child very lucky too – not only are they unique, but they literally have a one-of-a-kind mother. That is something to cherish and celebrate, so take a moment to do just that. Your parenting style will be unique and that's completely OK.

Embrace the imperfections and not knowing the right move

Your aim isn't to be perfect and getting it right all the time; it's about learning and supporting one another. Just remember, you didn't know what to do months ago, or a year ago or even yesterday, but you found a way that worked and you will continue to find ways. It's OK if some take longer than others; there's no rush and it's not a race.

Emotion

Tears and hair-pulling moments are part of the process; however, getting consumed by it won't serve any purpose. If this occurs, take deep breaths in and out, and gently take a moment to observe the scene and your thoughts, then observe again and this time without any judgement. At this point I then repeat my favourite affirmation – "I AM ENOUGH" – because whatever is happening is really not a big deal. Thousands of mums have been in this exact situation before you and thousands more will follow. Simply by taking a moment to stop, witness and observe without judgement, followed by positive affirmations, allows the mind to become relaxed and focused once more.

Comparing-itis

You don't need to be dressed immaculately, provide a wholesome packed lunch, win the sports race, or be on the PTA team to feel like the best mum or look like a good parent. The love, laughter and memories you create as a family is the feel-good factor you need. When you begin to look inwards, focusing on the outward things will stop becoming a priority. It's very easy to look at others, compare and make yourself feel bad if they appear to be doing more. However, think about this for a moment – does it make you feel better? Do you become a better mum by feeling inadequate? No? So, again, if it's not serving a purpose, there's no reason to do it. Be mindful of your thoughts and when comparing-itis occurs, observe but give it no attention. Instead, give that energy to yourself, to your family and choose to see love for who you all are as a unit. If you feel judged by others, see it as reflection on them and not you.

Work on the inner warrior

Develop your love and strength from within and start believing that you are a fabulous and beautiful mum. Remind yourself every morning and every evening how incredible you are, what an amazing mother you are, how you are learning so much every day, and that you embrace any imperfections that may arise. In life we are often given rules and procedures to follow, starting at school, in a new job, how to buy a house and even antenatal classes. The one time there is no handbook, terms and conditions, right or wrong is when it comes to parenting. Be kind, be patient, be forgiving, not just for your child but for YOU. We tell the kids to simply try their best and not to worry about any setbacks but to simply learn from them; we can use the same advice for ourselves. Enjoy the ride of being the perfectly imperfect parent.

You can't always control
what life gives but you can
control how you respond
to life

Nourish

Curl Up and Eat Cake Time
– Courgette and Lemon Cake
with Cashew Icing

My absolutely favourite thing to do at the end of a hectic day like this is to simply curl up on the sofa, put a reality TV show on (my guilty pleasure) and eat cake! I don't particularly want to be the midnight-munchies mum or morning-after-guilty mum, so of course it has to be my favourite courgette and lemon cake with cashew icing.

You can even give a slice of this to the kids for breakfast and totally rock being the cool mum!

Recipe

Cake Ingredients

- 1 cup spelt flour
- 1 cup ground almonds
- 2 medium courgettes
- 1 lemon juiced
- ¼ cup coconut oil
- ½ teaspoon baking powder
- 1 teaspoon allspice/cinnamon
- Pinch of pink salt

Cake Method

1. Blitz the courgettes in a food processor.
2. Add the flour, almonds, baking powder, spices and salt, and mix.
3. Add the lemon and coconut oil and mix a final time before placing in a silicone loaf tray and baking for thirty to thirty-five minutes at 180 degrees.

Icing Ingredients

- 1 cup cashews soaked overnight or ten minutes in hot water
- 3 tablespoons of agave or maple syrup
- 2 tablespoons of lemon juice

Icing Method

1. Blitz the above in the food processor ready to ice the top of the cake once it's out of the oven and cooled.
2. Store in the fridge for one week.

Yoga Pose

Warrior 1 Pose

Let's change the worrier to warrior; the warrior pose is perfect for this frame of mind.

It is aimed at allowing you to feel strong, brave and ready to take on the world.

Direction

1. Stand in mountain pose.
2. Step your right foot towards the back of your mat, creating a long stance.
3. Turn your right heel down and angle your foot at forty-five degrees.
4. Bend your left knee as close to ninety degrees as you can.
5. Extend both arms upwards.
6. Try and angle both hips towards the front – shoulders to the front, hips angled at forty-five degrees.
7. Hold for five breaths before returning to mountain pose and repeating on the other side.

Benefits

- Strengthens upper and lower body.
- Strengthens weak muscles.
- Builds endurance and provides energy perfect for when the mind is feeling a little fragile.

THREE

What's for Dinner Mum

How was your day? Good… what's for dinner? This was the standard question and response I got for days on end. If it was the weekend, during breakfast I would get asked what's for lunch; whilst munching through lunch they would ask what's for dinner. Creating weekly menus and shopping lists seemed never-ending. Ensuring meals are colourful, nutritious and appetising, and trying not to feel guilty when I could only squeeze in beans on toast after school or before the dash to swimming club was my weekly saga.

Of course you want to cook healthy, wholesome meals, with lots of vegetables and other nutrients. You want it to include all food groups and have rainbow colours and taste amazing. You want to be the mum whose house is wafting with smells of freshly baked treats, children who love all your food and washing-up that simply disappears.

However, when you factor in time, fussy eaters, cost, loving or loathing cooking itself, convenience, slow eaters, and everything in between, it really can seem like every parent's nightmare. Often with so much material available to us, whether we search for it or we see it on social media, it can add pressure. Should we be going organic? Plant-based? I only had time to go to the supermarket and bought apples covered in plastic – am I an awful mum? Is rice carcinogenic, and if so, what have I done giving my child rice crackers? Grains or no grains? More avocados? I don't even like avocados! Arrggghhhhh! It can be so hard knowing what to do, and then finding the time to do it, and doing it perfectly right?

One thing we do know is that we need to eat! We need to stay nourished and we usually aim to do this a few times a day. Keeping it simple is key.

Mindfulness and Motivation Tips

Keep it simple

I can tell you right now, you can take a big deep breath in and just let all those food worries goooooo.

Take that pressure right off yourself. You do not need to be creating gourmet-style dinners every day, or any day, and it really is OK to have a day where frozen food simply goes into the oven and comes out, ready to eat. This is the way it should be, leading your most perfectly imperfect life and being absolutely OK with it.

Energetic child says it all

Have a look at your child; do you think they have grown since six months ago? Are they full of energy and constantly on the go? Then I can guarantee your culinary skills are absolutely fine.

Now, I absolutely love cooking – however, many people don't, and that is OK too. You don't have to love everything and be good at it to be able to still deliver. Stir-frying some vegetables, boiling some peas, washing some fruit to create a fruit salad and filling some pre-made wraps is more than fine – simple yet effective (beans on toast, cheese toasties – also totally fine).

Mindful eating

This is the perfect time to practise mindful eating at your next meal too. Whatever is on your plate in the next meal, have a look at it as if you have never seen it before. Explore the colours, shape and texture just by looking at it. Do the same again when you put it in your mouth, but this time with taste and feeling it. Let it sit on your tongue for a moment, slowly take your time and really savour each mouthful. Just for twenty minutes, enjoy the food without being distracted by anything such as the TV, jobs or distracting thoughts.

When you want to go deeper, think about where the food came from and how it ended up on your plate. Think of the people that may have grown the food, given it the love and energy, to those that may have packaged it and that may have delivered it to where you bought it. There's a whole story and journey to what you are eating. This will really allow you to appreciate the meal, the food, and you'll enjoy the experience that much more and will actually come away feeling fuller.

A completely different experience compared to if you were on the go, multi-tasking or being distracted whilst eating. This is perfect for the kids to do with you and have a conversation about. Asking them which country they think a particular fruit is from? Or how many ingredients are in a particular meal? They, too, will appreciate the value of the food that much more.

You don't need to do this at every mealtime, every single day (I know time is of the essence a lot of the time), but factoring it in on some occasions will have a huge impact on mealtimes.

Sprinkle a little love onto every meal

When meals are created with love instead of a means to an end, the mealtimes will become something to look forward to, and a more enriched experience. Take the kids shopping and allow them to enjoy all the abundance of food available; ask them, if they could pick two fruits or vegetables, what would they be? Ask them to pick one vegetable that they have never tried before and that could be the family vegetable challenge of the week. Allow them to get involved with menus and ideas, new recipes and even shopping lists, and ask them to calculate how much things would cost.

The more mindful they are in knowing what goes into a meal, from shopping, costs, recipes and creating, they will grow to appreciate the meals they are having rather than wondering what the next one will be. Conscious cooking, creating and eating can really make a huge difference.

Meals stuffed with gratitude, topped with love and a side of food for thought

Allow gratitude to be a big part of cooking and making meals. The abundance of food and choices available, the ability to be able to select and pick from such a variety, the endless colours that are displayed in the shops, and the ready recipes and ingredients that are now even sent to us in the post, should we wish. Know that your child has continued to grow and develop from the day they were born, because you have fed them not with just physical food but with so much love. The love you give is the greatest nourishment that children can ever receive.

Take a moment to be grateful to yourself that you have managed to put meals on a plate for your child for x amount of years without fail. You have never missed or forgotten a meal (forgetting packed lunches doesn't count, as I'm sure your school didn't allow them to starve!). Whether that was cereal for dinner one day or a lasagne packed with 101 vegetables, the fact that you always have something to provide with lashings and toppings of love is all that matters. So the next time your child asks, "What's for dinner?", tell them, "Nothing but love."

Nourish

Pasta with Vegetables

This is the definite go-to meal for my family; when I don't know what to make, pasta usually comes to the rescue. It's warm, filling and I can definitely sneak a few extra vegetables in.

Recipe

Ingredients

- 4 ripe tomatoes
- ½ courgette chopped
- 4 broccoli florets chopped
- 1 box of passatta
- Dried oregano
- 1 teaspoon pink salt
- 2 garlic cloves
- 1 teaspoon of coconut sugar (optional)
- Pasta of your choice (we love lentil pastas; but there are so many out there from wholewheat, red lentil, black bean, chickpea, edamame and much more)
- 2 tablespoons of oil (I use coconut oil)

Method

1. Heat the oil.
2. Add in the garlic for a couple of minutes.
3. Add the tomatoes and other veg.
4. Add the passata.
5. Add salt, sugar and oregano and let it cook for ten minutes.
6. I then scoop it all in my blender and blitz for a smooth sauce to serve with the precooked pasta.
7. Optional: add cheese/chilli flakes/pesto.
8. Optional: add a side of cooked mushrooms, spinach, sweetcorn or olives. I leave them in little bowls on the table so the kids can help themselves.

Yoga Pose

Tree Pose

This pose allows grounding and focus and standing strong. Focus on the love and nourishment you provide in the meals you create for your children. Like a tree weathering all seasons and staying strong in the roots, you too can stay true to the fact that as long as the food is made with love, that is all that matters. With this as the focus, you can relax and know you are all growing and staying strong, just like the pose of the tree.

Direction

1. Standing in mountain pose.
2. Shift your weight slightly on to the left foot.
3. Bend the right knee and lift, open your hips, then take the right foot up and place the sole on the inner left ankle or inner left calf with toes facing down (advance movement to lift to inner thigh and using hand to lift the foot to help stabilise you).
4. Rest your hands on your pelvis.
5. Lengthen your tailbone and fixate your gaze at a point in front of you.
6. Stay here for a few breaths, before returning to mountain pose and repeating for the other side.
7. Adaptation: stand with your back against a wall if you are feeling unsteady.

Benefits

- Improves balance
- Relieves sciatica
- Strengthens muscles in the legs and back

FOUR

Taxi Mum

You are picking the kids up from school: today is gymnastics club, tomorrow swimming, the next day choir, at the weekend it's dancing in the morning followed by a playdate and Sunday it's two birthday parties for both kids in different directions. Does this sound like a typical week? Running from one place to another, water bottles and snacks on the go, seatbelts fastening and unfastening. As much as the kids love the activities – and of course you do too – the preparation that goes on behind the scenes NO ONE WILL EVER KNOW!

Dinner before or after the club? Which snacks won't look like I'm the mum giving my kids a sugar rush? Are they actually learning anything? (Come on, you must question that too sometimes? No, just me?) Do I even want to look at how much this is costing me? Can they fit into the costume/uniform for a few more weeks? If you have more than one child, then that's even more time gone with different schedules. One child likes football, the other wants to try piano, you secretly want them to be dancers (probably more because the thought of standing outside in the cold or listening to recitals all year long isn't very appealing).

I used to recall not liking days simply because they were chaotic; it would be terrible Tuesday or frantic Friday. Every week I dreaded these days. The thought of it would tire me out mentally more than the physical activity. Especially in the winter months, I would come home from the school pick-up and wish it would be a non-club day. I didn't want to go through the after-school quick hustle bustle and turn around to the next activity.

It came to a point where I thought, *I cannot change the schedule, but I can change how I react towards it. I can make it as fun and interesting as I want or let it be something I struggle to get through.* Our minds are constantly registering what day it is and where we need to be, and whilst going or arriving at the destination we are then thinking what we need to do next. Everything feels like effort and stress; often this can be picked up by the kids too. However, we can change that, and enjoy the chaos and find the calm in it.

Mindfulness and Motivation Tips

Enjoy the ride

Enjoy the journey that you are going on; the taxi runs aren't going to stop anytime soon, so take a moment to enjoy the ride. When you are driving, take in the surroundings through all the senses. Notice the colours around you, the shifting clouds, the changing seasons, the cars in front of you and the scenery as you stop at the traffic lights. Let go of any thoughts, apart from what's there in front of you (don't worry about the mess at home you need to return to, or the milk you've forgotten to buy for tomorrow). Enjoy the scenery (no, I don't live on a tropical island). There really is beauty in everything if you take a moment to look for it.

Mindful driving

Take a moment to feel the seat you are sitting on, the steering wheel your hands are on, the appreciation that you are able to drive this machine and go from one place to another. You are able to transport not just yourself but your child/children to their activities. Listen to the sounds around you – whether it's the music, the children talking or anything going on outside. Take a moment to really listen to the children, how their vocabulary may be changing, their knowledge, their observations and their questions. How they have changed from only a year ago. I recall always trying to keep my child awake on the return journey home when she was younger, and now we have the cutest conversations. I love engaging with them, especially with all the random, weird and wonderful things they come out with.

Take it as an opportunity to bond with the kids, talk to them about what they love about their activity, any new friends they have made or even playing a game of who can spot the 'green car' first. I won't forget the time my daughter reached home and said, "I enjoyed talking to you, Mummy."

Home is where the heart is

In between journeys, take a moment to appreciate your home, the shelter and relief it provides to all of you. It may be for a short time in between trips, but enjoy the comfort it gives you all.

Use your time productively

If you are waiting at the club/activity for your child, again practise mindfulness, enhance your senses by really noticing your surroundings. Enjoy watching your child, listen to the sounds or take a moment to absorb the atmosphere. A place where your child feels safe, has fun, smiles, makes friends and learns new skills. Take it as an opportunity to also practise gratitude that your child/children have so much opportunity to learn, grow and play. Take a moment for yourself to acknowledge that due to your love, care and wanting the best for your child, they are experiencing great opportunities.

The benefit of doing the above is it will give you a moment to practise gratitude and appreciate the small things often taken for granted. As a result, you will soften your thoughts, feel more relaxed, any impatience will be reduced and you will begin to enjoy the experience that much more.

Opportunity for ME TIME

Practising mindfulness is important, but also if you do have that waiting period whilst an activity finishes, use that for some 'me time'. Use that thirty minutes for YOU: read a book, go for a walk, write in a journal, do something that is about you. I used to aimlessly scroll on and off social media in between staring into space whilst I waited for my daughter's class to end. I then made a decision to use the time proactively. I began walking around the block during the summer, bringing a good book in when it was winter and even meeting a friend for coffee during longer sessions. I felt grateful that my children had so many activities available to them and began to embrace the journey that was attached to them.

Nourish

Chocolate Energy Balls

The perfect on-the-go snack has to be energy balls; they are small yet powerful enough to have an impact. They taste indulgent and continue to release energy; my kids and I absolutely love these and I know you will too. Have fun with these and get the kids to experiment too, I have literally just eaten two whilst typing away... yum yum.

Recipe

Ingredients

- 1 cup oats (gluten-free if you prefer)
- 1 cup ground almonds
- ½ cup cacao powder
- ½ cup coconut oil
- 3 tablespoons chia seeds
- 1/3 cup maple syrup/agave
- (Optional fine coconut)

Method

1. Mix it all in a food processor and roll into balls.
2. Leave to set in the fridge for ten minutes.
3. These last for three weeks in the fridge.
4. You can have so much fun with energy balls and if you choose to, then get the kids involved (or you may want to simply indulge in the deliciousness of it all for yourself).
5. Before allowing them to set in the fridge you can even coat them in seeds, fine coconut or cacao powder.
6. You can even experiment and add other ingredients in such as dried fruit, chocolate chips and seeds.

Yoga Pose

Lunge and Twist Pose

This pose allows you to see things from a different view, instead of seeing the taxi journey as A to B, you can now see it from different angles and take in observations you had never previously noticed.

Direction

Begin in a downward dog position, by coming on all fours, and then as you breathe in, lift your hips up and knees off the floor. Bring your heels towards the floor and let your head hang, looking down (see chapter 10 for image).

From this position, lift the right leg up, move forward into plank; whilst lunging the leg through the hands, keep looking forward to the hands. As you step the right foot forward, make any further adjustments to get to this position.

Extend your right arm towards the ceiling and look up (twist and reach out to the side until the arm is vertical).

Open your chest and draw your shoulders down, keeping a straight line through your right arm. Breathe for three deep breaths and step back into plank. Take a moment before making back into plank, then downward dog and continuing on to the other side.

Adaptation: Bring your knees to the mat if you are unable to straighten your legs.

Benefits

- Stretches your spine.
- Increases mobility.
- Detoxifies internal organs.
- By opening up your body to a new direction, you can open up your mind too.

FIVE

Mum Tum

The Mum Body

OK, so we have all heard that it takes nine months to produce the baby so we should allow nine months to regain our figure. Yes, we all have the occasional thought that once we have given birth we are going to be one of those mums that looks incredible straight after, the one where we pretend that's just how we naturally look and no effort whatsoever was made before visitors were allowed to enter the vicinity (a perfect messy bun and lots of natural make-up was of course not part of any plan).

We may entertain thoughts of being the mum where they use the baby as weights, incorporating the baby into the exercise and see it as a bonding exercise, done and seen so many times on Instagram and YouTube. You may even think that despite the tiredness and chaotic days, you will not sleep when the baby sleeps, you will not rest when your child's at school, you will not wind down in the evening, instead you will use one of those times to do a workout.

If you are one of those mums, I totally salute you and admire you; at times I used to be the mum who would fit in a thirty-minute workout when my daughter had a morning nap... I would also be the mum that on the same day scoffed a whole heap of chocolate in the evening in less than thirty minutes.

Our days are more preoccupied, our schedule is definitely busier, we can be more tired and there is always the dilemma of coffee and break time or workout time.

Months or years can really fly and sometimes our body doesn't spring back into pre-mum shape (sometimes it totally can), despite our best efforts. Whether we choose to work out, or have the best intentions to and life gets in the way, it's very easy to pass the mirror and be self-critical. The still ever so slight or very large muffin top, the slightly squishier skin, the circles under the eyes (or, as my husband likes to call them, suitcases) and all the other imperfections, we may see. I know mum friends who are super lean and still only notice the imperfections.

I for one lost the weight after my first child; however, this was not the case after the second child. Was it because I had two C-sections? (That couldn't be it, because Victoria Beckham had four.) Had my metabolism slowed down after I tried the cabbage soup diet? Was my system messed up after trying paleo, keto and every other way of eating? I don't know and never will; all I do know is that my children see strength when they see me and the only shape they see me when they look at me is a mummy-looking one.

As humans we are very quick to self-judge and criticise. We find it far easier to see the imperfections than we do our perfections. We would often readily and just as quickly accept criticism from others as we would if they were paying us a compliment. However, we would also be the first to oppose comments if someone else was being critical towards themselves.

Your body became a home

I am going to get the first tip out of the way because I know you may have heard it before, but this time I really want you to take a moment (maybe even close your eyes) and really believe what I am about to say next. Once upon a time, a beautiful miracle formed inside of you. Take your eyes inwards and think of all the work your body did to give your child its first home. A home inside of you that created warmth, nourishment and security. You did that not for a day, or a week, but many months whilst still going about your day-to-day life. That's a huge thing you did for another being, and as you remember feeling so much love for that child that was growing inside of you, give that same love to your body right now.

Gratitude body scan

Take ten minutes to either sit or lay down. Gently close your eyes and focus on your breath, inhaling slowly and exhaling slowly. Any distracting thoughts that appear, let them come, but don't give it any attention and simply focus back on your breath. Slowly start paying attention to the different parts of your body, starting from your feet all the way to your head. Each time you are focused on a body part, let it know how grateful you are for it being there and supporting you to its best ability. When you have completed this, take a few breaths and gently open your eyes; this will allow you to start focusing on positive thoughts towards your body.

Mindful language

Your children will always look up to you (even if it doesn't always feel that way) and will mirror your behaviour over time (although mine are still yet to mirror me when I keep on cleaning the bathroom sink). Show them that beauty and strength come from within. Be mindful not to be constantly looking in the mirror asking yourself, *Do I look big/OK in this?* Be mindful not to always show your body insecurities in front of your children. Be mindful not to say, "Mum's on a diet, so I can't eat that." Simply be mindful of your language and maybe even change your dialogue when you catch yourself having imperfect thoughts.

Your best shape is being a mummy shape

Be healthy as a family and involve the kids in your healthy plans. Maybe choose meals together, talk about the ingredients; if you choose to do a workout, maybe they can join in, or it could be something fun like skipping or catching a ball together. Embrace the person that you are right now in that moment, the mum with many different hats. Love your shape, size and imperfections for exactly what they are right now. Think about how much this physical part of you has got you through life. The legs for running after the kids, the hands to create meals, the eyes to see they are always OK, the ears to hear the laughter and tears, the whole body for feeling theirs when you get that amazing hug. If and when you are ready to make further changes, then slowly start implementing them: the short walk, the first exercise class booking, the friend you call to go to yoga with you, the new cookbook you buy, etc. Small changes for long-term maintenance, the key being that there is no pressure. You are perfectly imperfect.

'You're braver than you believe, and stronger than you seem, and smarter than you think'
Christopher Robin

Nourish

Colourful Wraps

I absolutely love making wraps. If we have time then I love having all the ingredients laid out on the table so the kids can create their own wrap – although it's not quite so fun when my youngest will stuff it to the brim and expect me to neatly fold it.

Recipe

Ingredients
There are many wraps available in the supermarket that add nutrition and colour; from beetroot, spinach and sweet potato wraps, and most of these are gluten-free too.

- 1 can pinto or kidney beans
- Lettuce
- 2 carrots
- 3 tomatoes
- Cucumber
- 2 bell peppers
- Hummus (ready-bought or recipe available)
- Optional add-ons: salsa, guacamole or olives
- Pink Salt
- Pepper

Method

1. This is fairly straightforward: simply shred the lettuce, grate the carrots and dice the tomatoes, cucumber and peppers.
2. Mix all in a bowl.
3. Add the pre-rinsed beans.
4. Add a little pink salt and pepper.
5. Spread the hummus on the wrap, fill the wrap with the salad; roll, wrap and eat.

Hummus Ingredients

- 1 can of chickpeas washed and dried or 250g precooked chickpeas (if using the dried version)
- 1 large lemon juiced
- 3 tablespoons tahini
- 2 tablespoons extra virgin oil
- ½ teaspoon cumin
- Pink salt for taste
- 3 tablespoons water (more if required)

Hummus Method

1. In a food processor, blend the tahini with the lemon juice and cumin.
2. Add the oil and salt, and blitz for thirty seconds.
3. Add the chickpeas, blend again for thirty seconds, stop, scrape the side, add water and blend again for two minutes.
4. Add extra water if too thick.
5. Optional: add ½ red pepper chopped, a few sundried tomatoes or even some coriander to create different flavour hummus.

Yoga Pose

Triangle Pose

We are all different shapes and sizes; that's what makes us so unique. We often want to be the thing that we are not, but when we embrace our imperfections we start to love the person we are and beauty always comes from within. Speaking of shapes, a triangle shape is as good as any.

Direction

1. Stand in a mountain pose.
2. Spread your feet wider than your hips. (To get an idea how far the legs need to be, spread your hand out at shoulder height; the feet need to the same distance at the wrists.)
3. Turn both feet to the right and whilst keeping the legs straight, reach the right arm and torso to the right as far as possible — both knees remain straight.
4. Once at maximum stretch, the right hand lowers towards the shin or ankle and the left hand reaches up vertically.
5. To make things easier, look down or look up to make it a little advanced.
6. Check you are in line and in alignment.

Benefits

- Improves balance, digestion and fires up the core
- Reduces blood pressure, stress and anxiety.

SIX

Losing My Identity Mum

We were all someone before we became a mum; in fact, I am pretty sure I had another name? We have all had various other titles in the past – from daughter, sister, niece, friend, employee, colleague – and that's OK because they just show the position we hold in someone's life. It didn't define us as a person, as such. I was still the [*whichever title*], who was a yoga lover, spa break finder, afternoon tea eater, and enjoyed reading and having downtime.

When motherhood began, I became the mum, but was also now a cook, cleaner, coach, creator, baker, painter, decorator, accountant and everything in between. Every single day consisted of more than one of these jobs, and it was a case of which hat am I wearing for this hour?

The world centres around our child/ren and of course they are our world, but sometimes when we become so consumed in looking after them and their needs, we can often forget to look after ourselves and our own needs. Often we don't know where we begin and they end. Our lives become so entwined it's hard to see past what needs doing next for them.

I know that a lot of my week is filled with constant times and dates for whatever is going on for my kids and what I need to bring to where and when. Is it homework day, dress up at school day, parents' evening, club competition, class assembly, show rehearsals, etc. Then there are the appointments for the hairdressers, opticians, dentists, buying more school shoes, parties and playdates. I actually feel like I am constantly in one of those revolving doors. Oh, not to forget that between all this the meals need to be made, laundry done, and make sure that the toilet roll and toothpaste never run out. Plus, is it me or does a big part of the day revolve around picking the food up from under the table on the kitchen floor? (I don't even have any pets!) I am pretty sure you could feed a small country with the amount of food that ends up there!

With so much going on, it really can be easy to lose who we are as an individual. Who are we without the entourage? What do we like doing? Can we even have a conversation without bringing our children into it? Who are you without the label or a role to play? It is really important to keep who you are alive and kicking; at the centre of everything you do, don't forget to be YOU.

Mindfulness and Motivation Tips

Self-love

Stop for a moment and simply close your eyes (after reading the rest of the sentence), and repeat, "I am [*your name*] and I love [*list all the things you love, including hobbies, foods, movies, etc.*]." Really take a moment to feel and become that person once again; feel who you are without any role or title. Reconnect with who you are once again.

Self-care

Now you may already enjoy the occasional night out with friends or other social gatherings, but it's important to also spend time with just yourself. You may think, why on earth would you want to do that? But it's really vital to get to know yourself, to know the person you are without the role. What is it like to do things without being in mum, friend or work mode? Take time to read, listen to music, create something crafty, watch a movie or go for a jog; whatever it is, take the time to spend with your thoughts. Be really mindful when you do this, try not to be distracted with the to-do list, and really give one hundred per cent of your thoughts and energy to whatever it is you are doing. It may also feel a little strange to do this if you haven't done it already – a little quiet when you are used to so much background noise – and that's even more reason to begin enjoying your own company.

Social interaction

Create space in the month to connect with your friends and family. Playdates and school-related activities may take up the diary, but make space for just adult time. It could be a regular class you attend, from a fitness-related one, to a book club, a wine club or even a walk. It could be a dinner date or a night at the cinema; whatever it is, make sure you have something in the diary. It may even be inviting friends over for a pizza and a movie if the thought of going out isn't always appealing, especially as JOMO (joy of missing out) is trendier than FOMO (fear of missing out) at the moment.

Mummy has a life too

Introduce your children to your personality; let them be a part of who you are as much as you are a part of them. You may get involved in playing Lego with them to really being part of their next homework project; you may take them clothes shopping or be cheering them on at their next show, but let them have that same role in your life. If previously you liked drawing or creating things, then start again and let them do it too; if you liked visiting certain places, either take them or, if that's another stress, show them pictures and talk about it. Show them the music you listened to or photos of your previous adventures. Find a way of joining the two worlds in whichever way you can.

Nourish

Pizza

Pre-motherhood or during motherhood, we all like to have a slice of pizza, and usually that's the one thing you will all enjoy. It can be fun, creative and colourful, and if it's like my family, individual pizzas show the individual personalities (mushroom on one, olives on another, extra sweetcorn for everyone).

Recipe

Ingredients
Base

- 3 cups spelt flour
- 1 cup warm water
- 1 tablespoon Salt
- 1 tablespoon olive oil
- 1 tablespoon yeast

Sauce

- 1 box of passata
- 1 tablespoon coconut sugar
- 1 teaspoon pink salt
- 2 tablespoons olive oil
- 2 cloves garlic
- 1 tablespoon mixed herbs
- Pizza topping of choice (peppers, spinach, olives, mushrooms, jalapenos, sweetcorn, roasted vegetables)

Method
Base

1. Mix 1 cup of the flour, water and yeast in a bowl, and let it set for twenty minutes
2. Stir in the remaining flour, olive oil and salt.
3. Mix and knead the flour until a soft dough forms. Leave the dough to set for forty-five minutes.
4. Separate the dough into two, and then roll out into a base.

Sauce

1. Heat the oil, add the garlic. After a few minutes, add the passata, sugar and salt; continue to heat for ten minutes.
2. Add the sauce onto the base, add toppings of choice, garnish with mixed herbs and bake in the oven for twenty-five minutes.

Yoga Pose

Bridge Pose

Often, simply lying down and taking a moment can help us feel grounded and give us clarity. We are always looking around us; take a moment to look up and find peace on the ceiling. Let it represent a blank canvas where you can create anything.

Directions

1. Lie down on your back, palms resting on the side, feet flat on the floor with knees bent. Keep feet parallel and hip width apart.
2. On exhale, press the floor away from your feet and lift the hips gently off the floor (squeeze the glutes). Stay for a few breaths, then lift your heels up and slowly lower your hips back to the ground, one vertebra at a time. Repeat five times.

Benefits

- This is an energising stretch of the lower back and mobilises the spine, also opening the chest and heart; it can also calm the mind and reduce anxiety.

SEVEN

Shouty Mum

OK, we have all been there: a certain situation arises with the kids, you tell yourself you are going to be calm and patient, you will talk gently, you will not lose your mind… definitely not this time… and the next minute you see red and that's it; your mouth opens and a whole flurry of words escapes at such a volume that you are pretty sure it's triggered an earthquake. For some reason you can't seem to close your mouth and the words continue to flow out, until suddenly you feel this eerie silence descend upon you, which is what makes you stop for a minute. You notice a pair of eyes staring back at you, looking slightly scared, and then their eyes fill with water and spill out silently. (Either that or they yell just as loud and just as hard back.)

Then the worst feeling in the world takes over, which is guilt. It fills your body and you feel like the worst mum ever for losing your cool. You had promised yourself the last time that this wouldn't happen, you feel like you are the only one who acts like this – I mean, there is no way any of the school mums would ever lose their cool – and your thoughts on failing parenthood begin to spiral.

Now I will stop you there to tell you the one simple fact that you really aren't the only one to ever yell at your child; every parent has pretty much had a moment of reacting in the same way, and I for one didn't know how to manage my own awareness and control before practising mindfulness and would react in the same way many, many times. I always felt like this psycho mum because my temper would just go at the smallest things. I felt like I had no patience... ever!

However, I knew also that this couldn't be the only way. I was sure I could absolutely control my reaction to any situation. I didn't need to shout or yell to have an impact (unless, of course, they were about to put their hands in the socket or something), I didn't need to continue to raise my voice to get their attention, and I certainly didn't need them mirroring my reaction in the future.

I can honestly say that after practising mindfulness and working on my inner calm, I really don't feel it's necessary to raise my voice to show them I mean business. It feels good to have this control, and it feels good to work through situations in a much calmer environment. This calmness over my tone, mood and patience has made one of the biggest differences to me personally and, of course, to my family.

Mindfulness and Motivation Tips

Take a deep breath

Deep breathing is extremely powerful here; breathing deeply right into your stomach and slowly exhaling (minimum ten breaths) will slow your heart rate down and will signal for the brain to calm down too. This in turn will get you out of the fight/flight reflex and instead allow you to think clearly and logically. It will give you that space and time to respond and not react.

Find a space

Instead of telling your children to stop or go somewhere, remove yourself from the situation for a few minutes. Go to a different room or on the stairs and continue to breathe deeply. This will remove you from the triggers that are getting your emotions to rise.

Ask the question

Explain to your child what it is about their behaviour that they could improve on, what it is that you were not happy with and how it made you feel. Often when a child sees the impact it has on you, this is when they will rethink their actions next time. You could even start by asking them what they think they could have done differently. Often, when the answer comes from them, they are more likely to actually understand their behaviour and consequences. When we are quick to tell them, "You did x, y and z wrong," they are more likely to feel defensive and not feel understood; this in turn leaves no room for learning or moving forward. The process of calming them down will take longer because they will feel attacked or not believe their side will be heard, even if it's an apology.

Communication is key to calm

When the conversation has been had, tell them you feel proud that you were able to discuss it like a grown-up. Tell them this took good listening and communication skills. If things haven't resolved, tell them to maybe write down what it is they are feeling, I often tell my daughter to say, "I am feeling [*she fills in the word, e.g. frustrated, angry, sad*] because [*she thinks of the answer*]." It is a good way to express whatever it is they are feeling in the moment. If one or both of us are still feeling frustrated and we need extra time, we choose one of the following to do for a few minutes:

- Read,
- Listen to music,
- Doodle with pencil and paper,
- Write,
- Then, when we are ready, we come back together and have a little chat.

Accept it's OK to have moments like this, that things can go wrong and that's OK; the key is how you move forward from it. It's harder when it may be the same thing that's causing you to be frustrated (kids never doing the bed or tidying up, etc.). I have absolutely been there and still can be there on days, but I explain to them how it makes me feel, and by me spending extra time on something it takes out time for other things, such as playing or hanging out with them. Promote how working together to find solutions can benefit all of you and, as my daughter likes to remind me, the word POSSIBLE is in IMPOSSIBLE.

Nourish

Superlicious Fudge

This may be the time when you need something sweet and indulgent, and some fudge may just do the trick. Sometimes, when I do steal a moment for myself or even have some time with the kids, it's nice to munch over these little bites of pure yumminess.

Recipe

Ingredients
- 1 cup almond or cashew butter
- 1/3 cup coconut oil
- ½ cup cacao powder
- ½ cup agave or maple syrup
- 1 teaspoon pink salt

Method

1. Heat a pan on the lowest heat, and add the almond butter and coconut oil. Give it a good stir.
2. Add the cacao powder, maple syrup and pink salt.
3. Turn off the heat and continue to give it a good mix.
4. Line a small square tray with parchment paper and transfer the mixture in. Smooth the surface over with a spatula or knife.
5. Freeze for thirty minutes, then cut in squares and eat.
6. Keep in the fridge or keep in squares in the freezer if it is too soft.

Yoga Pose

Child's Pose

This is a great time to be just like a child and allow that release through child's pose.

Direction

1. Start on the floor on all fours, keeping your knees hip-width distance apart.
2. Breathe in, and as you breathe out, sink your bottom over your heels and place your forehead to the floor.
3. You can place your arms overhead with palms on the floor or along the side of your body, palms facing up.
4. Breathe slowly, pressing your tummy on your thigh and hold for a few breaths.
5. To release, place your palms under your shoulders and gently sit up.

Benefits

- Resting the forehead on the floor provides a calming effect on the brain straightaway.
- The position also gives a sense of being grounded and in balance with harmony.
- It also allows you to stretch your hips and thighs whilst reducing stress and fatigue.
- It relaxes the muscles of the front body and stretches the back torso as well.

EIGHT

Birthday Party Mum

Birthday parties used to be super cute and super easy (I hope you noted the words 'used to be'). Invite the class, most of the kids whom you didn't know (usually getting a list from the class teacher), go to a play area and drink cups of tea with parents... again, most of whom you don't know. You are guaranteed two things: 1) cake that you can eat for breakfast for the new few days and 2) your child will be exhausted and you can get your annual night's decent sleep.

As the kids get older, it's a whole different story; these birthday parties are turning into weddings with the amount of prep that goes into them! I have actually started dreading these events... even to the point that I'm willing to sacrifice the birthday cake! The planning itself takes the cake!

Planning begins two to three months beforehand.

Do the dates clash with anything?

Are the best friends available on those days?

Do I invite a smaller number of friends in an attempt to begin scaling down the thirty-people invite?

Do I invite a handful, but will someone feel left out? Will there be school politics about it the day after? Will other mums start hating on me that their child didn't make the list? Arrgghhh!

Where will it be this year, and is it enough to make my child think I'm a cool party mum?

Will it be a unicorns, princesses, pirates, sports or a fairies theme... you know, just so all the cutlery and napkins are matching.

What happened to buying a cake from the supermarket? Nope, now I have to show my child multiple pictures on Pinterest to see what design and flavours she would like before getting it ordered. It's posh food and mocktails, with more than one option of starter, main and dessert (which, of course, needs checking is OK with the kids beforehand) unless I can get away with a buffet. Then there's the party bags, party invites and, of course, the PARTY OUTFIT!

The other thing I find awkward is: do you tell parents to stay? (Does that then sound like you can't cope?) Do you tell them they can go? (Does that make them feel you don't want them there?) Do you just say nothing? The last option is the worst one for me, I have gone to parties before not knowing whether to stay or go; all of us parents are giving each other sideway glances, seeing what the next move is, hoping someone decides to exit so we can quickly all follow or we all slump in disappointment when this doesn't happen.

So yes, when the last guest leaves the party, I for sure am heaving a big sigh of relief.

You want to ensure your child has the best day because you know as they go to other people's parties the one they look most forward to is their own. However, finding the balance is key: do they need huge birthday parties every single year? With so much accessible and available, it's easy to get swept up in the moment, but is it sustainable year after year, and will the kids' expectations continue to increase? Again, it's hard to not feel judged if you do decide to scale things back. Will other children be mean to yours? Will they say their party was bigger and better? Will other parents begin to feel sorry for my child and wonder if you have some kind of financial issues or simply don't care? Do you just give in and go with it until they hit eighteen? What if? What if? What if?

You want it to be fun, you want it to be memorable and you just want to do it YOUR WAY.

Mindfulness and Motivation Tips

Reflect on the age they are nearing the end of

Whilst your child may be getting excited at the same time as your dread is creeping in towards the big day, spend some time together talking about the highlights of this age. What did they love about being the age they are right now; what cool and exciting things took place? What new things were they able to learn; can you share any of your memories with them of events that took place this year? Such as their first tooth falling out, or the zoo you visited, or when you visited Grandma and she made the best biscuits, etc. Spend time on enjoying their current age and let them know they won't be that age again so let's do some more x-year-old things first. It's nice that they look forward to the new age, but also, it's a good time for both of you to feel present with their current age and simply appreciate this moment.

What makes parties so cool?

What is it about their birthday that they love so much? Is it the idea or actually something specific? Often this isn't given actual thought and when I've asked my children, they have actually had to take a moment to think about it. Giving them this time to focus on WHY they love birthdays will allow the experience to be that much more enriched. This moment of sharing will also allow you to enjoy this part of their journey that much more.

Ask them what they remembered about their last party/ activity, if anything at all?

Was it the:

- Place,
- People,
- Cake,
- Presents,
- Certain moments?

Take a moment to reflect on these thoughts and feelings. The central focus is happiness, gratitude and celebration for a new age. Spend time and energy on focusing on what that really means for you and your child. Talk about it together. If the preparation takes a long time but the day goes by in a whirlwind, was it worth it when the memories are forgotten a week later? By looking at the parts that are important, this will help you to decide which to give more attention to, instead of trying to do everything and spreading yourself thin.

Being mindful together

Being mindful of the different parts of the event is really important, and sharing this part with your child is vital. Explain the effort that may have gone into different parts of the party; it will help them appreciate the work you have done so lovingly for them. Show how fortunate they are to be able to share the day with family or friends, have various themes to choose from and having a cake especially bought/made for such an important occasion. Enjoy each moment, the smile on their face, the cake stuck in their hair, the laughter, the sound of opening gifts, the morning of a date that won't be there again, the cup of tea at night as you sink on the sofa. Giving them a chance to appreciate their big day will make you feel that little bit more valued too (you will also be the best party mum in their eyes too).

Laugh at the things gone wrong

Embrace anything that goes wrong too; I've had times where balloons have flown into the sky just as I opened the car boot or a yellow cake arriving for a very pink-obsessed girl. It's these moments that change the day from ordinary to extraordinary, because you will survive these moments and laugh at them later. You can't change any mishaps, but you can absolutely control how you react to them.

Have fun and party

Really be present in the party; it's very easy to be constantly running around, being a good hostess, making sure everyone is happy, fed and watered. However, this can often lead to missing out on the actual experience and some beautiful moments. Get involved with the games, take an extra look at your child, sneak in an extra birthday cuddle and share a bit of big eyes moment when the birthday cake moment comes.

It will all be OK

Don't give every stage too much energy, enjoy the idea-planning, the cake-deciding and food menu. Have fun with it; when you notice any stress building up, simply observe it and then remind yourself that it's simply a party. However basic or crazy it is, there will definitely be fun and smiles. You have no one's judgement to worry about because you have a right to create the party the way you want to. Extravagant, simple and effective, outdoors, indoors, hired help, family help; whatever it is, it will be amazing because your energy and excitement will mirror your children's.

Nourish

Birthday Chocolate Cake

The best thing about birthdays is the food; you are guaranteed either a birthday breakfast that's exciting or worth running into the kitchen for, a well-thought-out birthday dinner where there are no limits or restrictions, but the moment everyone waits for is the birthday CAKE. This particular cake is the one you have been waiting all year for and which tastes different to all the rest. This one has meaning and significance, baked with fondness or bought with love. For this reason, I thought I would share with you an indulgent chocolate cake, one you can eat and not worry about feeling guilty about afterwards.

Recipe

Dry Ingredients
- 3 cups gluten-free flour (spelt flour if gluten is OK)
- 1 cup cacao powder
- Pinch of pink salt
- 2 teaspoons baking powder
- ¼ teaspoon sodium bicarbonate

Method
- Mix the above.

Wet Ingredients

- 1 cup almond milk or any nut milk of choice
- 1 cup water
- ½ cup melted coconut oil
- ½ cup maple syrup or agave

Method

1. Mix the above.
2. Mix the wet and dry ingredients together and mix/ whisk together.
3. Place in a round nine-inch cake tin and bake for about twenty minutes.
4. Test with the knife/toothpick and allow it to cool.
5. Option 1: keep as it is or make two cakes from the mixture and spread some frosting in the middle and top.
6. Option 2: cover the top with chocolate sauce, add fruit and nuts, and let it harden.

Bonus Chocolate Frosting Recipe

Ingredients

- 1 can coconut cream
- 1 tablespoon cacao powder
- 2 tablespoons agave

Method

1. Whisk all ingredients together and refridgerate for 30 minutes before applying to cake
2. This cake can last in the fridge for three weeks and makes a perfect breakfast treat too.

Yoga Pose

Kneeling Superman/Woman

You would definitely feel like the secret superhero at this party. Holding everything together and hosting multiple people takes a lot of skill, only ones that heroes have.

Direction

1. Come to the floor on all fours, your spine in neutral.
2. As you take a deep breath in, extend your right hand out in front of you and your left leg out behind you.
3. As you exhale, return to all fours.
4. As you inhale again, repeat for the other side.
5. Repeat this pattern a few times.

Benefits

- This will strengthen the lower and upper back, glutes and hamstrings, and also build core strength.
- A nice stretch after a busy day.

NINE

Laundry Mum

Not Another Pile of Laundry!

Does it always seem that laundry basket is completely full? (Is there a possibility that your kids put extra clothes in there simply to avoid folding and putting away clothes that are lying on the bedroom floor?) It can often seem OK to fill the machine with clothes, add the washing powder and turn the machine on, but by the time you have gotten round to folding and ironing this load (usually a week later), the next load is ready.

The worst things to fold are all the different pairs of socks, and it's guaranteed that even though you smugly counted the even pairs of socks that went in the wash, an odd number has come out. When the time does come that all the ironing is complete, clothes are put away and you feel that lovely 'mumsy' feeling of having done a good job, within twenty-four hours that clean school shirt has sauce spilt on it and there's mud on the shirts and trousers.

It's all the variations of washing as well: bed washing, towel washing, swim kit washing, other sports kits washing, general blacks, whites and colours washing. There is always some form of washing to do. It can seem like a never-ending repetitive task and often a thankless one.

Mindfulness and Motivation Tips

Clothes tell a story

When doing the laundry, take a moment to look at the clothes that are going in or coming out of the wash. The clothes that tell daily stories: the dancing leotard, the football shorts, the snuggly PJs, the school uniform; each and every item that holds a memory of that child and for you too.

See how the clothes are so unique and individual to the person who wears them, often representing their personality. The stains show food that was lovingly eaten (or wolfed down because it was so good) and the fun they have had running around living in the moment.

Comfort in clothes

Take note of the size of their clothes, and the colours and textures, how these have changed from months and years ago as their personality begins to take form and they grow older. Take in the fresh smells and the care you are giving the clothes when you feel them, knowing it is this that keeps the family warm, in comfort and continues their stories. These clothes provide comfort, protection and also shows their character.

Personality in clothes

My girls have very distinct personalities and dress sense, and often when I am folding their clothes I take a moment to treasure their favourite top or dress, knowing how much they love wearing it (over and over again, even though they have a thousand other choices), knowing it gives them some sort of confidence and security.

Multi-task opportunity

It's also a good time to get the steps and workout in, up and down the stairs or across the rooms, bending up and down, and not to mention the eyesight checker... where is the other sock?! If you are feeling eager when you are doing the laundry, maybe add in a few squats when loading the machine and a few more when unloading. You can also do this in between ironing the clothes, such as doing five squats between each iron... they do say mums can multi-task... or you can just watch Netflix... no judgement or pressure; the choice is yours and always yours to make.

Nourish

Snow White Coconut Balls

When you think of laundry, it's easy to also think of clean white clothes, so here is a beautiful recipe for pure white coconut balls. These are super simple to make and any mess won't even be noticeable. The perfect go-to treat during the whole laundry process and after.

Recipe

Ingredients

- 1 creamed coconut bar
- 2 cups coconut powder
- 7 tablespoons coconut butter or oil
- 4 tablespoons maple syrup/agave

Method

1. Melt the creamed coconut (do this by placing the unopened packet in hot water).
2. Stir in the coconut powder.
3. Add the sweetener.
4. Add the oil or butter.
5. Mix together (more oil/or butter may be required).
6. Roll into balls.
7. Keep in the fridge for twenty minutes and then eat away.

Yoga Pose

Chair Pose

Similar to a squat style, but this will allow you to remain in this position for a few minutes longer. Doing the laundry involves a bit of a journey, from getting the clothes, doing the laundry, ironing, folding and putting them away. The chair pose is the antidote to all the moving.

Direction

1. Stand straight with your feet touching side by side (or shoulder width).
2. Gently lower down as if you are about to sit on a chair, push the bottom back and gently bend the knees.
3. Hold the position and raise your hands upwards.
4. Hold for a few breaths.

Benefits

- This will activate the core and legs, which will help if you are going up and down when loading and unloading the machines.
- It also challenges your mind to stay present and positive.

TEN

School Holiday Mum Part 1

How Many Half-Term Breaks Are There?!

This particular one makes me laugh, because when I speak to other mums they are already on any numb-inducing products they can find (usually wine)… before the holidays have even begun! This anxiety over what's coming ahead fills any parent with… how do I put this… FEAR! Now I admit it is a military operation with so many things to consider, and yes, as much as spontaneity and going with the flow is great, it can often leave you rocking in the corner by the end. Now I will be perfectly honest, I do love the holidays and spending time with the kids, but that wasn't always the case and there are still times that I will want to pull out my hair. I, as most others, need to consider the following:

- Is there someone who will be looking after my child during the holidays if it isn't me?
- Have we booked time out to go away somewhere, whether it's camping in the garden to a seaside trip, often last-minute trips may cause more stress than ease?
- Schedule in days where there's nothing in the schedule, have days that involve no plans.
- Do their summer clothes still fit? I'm putting this in there because I was packing for our trip away and I couldn't find one dress that would fit my daughter (in my mind, I thought she had plenty in her cupboard and now I am going to have to face all the other shoppers out there!).
- Do we have enough food in the house? Because the same rules as school of one meal and one snack during the hours of 9-3 don't appear to be valid in holidays as they are in school.
- This is the UK, so have back-up indoor rainy game ideas, because as much as we would like to think we can sip cocktails whilst the kids entertain themselves in the garden, this won't always be the case.

Mindfulness and Motivation Tips

Mindful playing

Now what will they do during the one- or two-week holidays? This is the question that causes the panic and fear, because often the activities you may have had planned during the length of the holidays may last you just one day! Now I'll show my age here, because 'back in my day' we didn't need so many things to keep us entertained; we somehow found a way to do it ourselves.

Kids are very stimulated these days because so much is available to them. It is a good idea to strip that back and allow them to find their own way of being stimulated that doesn't necessarily involve a form of gadget. I often tell my girls that they are super lucky to have time at home to play whatever they want, whether it's with their toys, crafts, books, etc. It allows them to be still for a moment, instead of thinking of the next thing, and appreciate the activities they have in abundance around them. I don't give them any further suggestions and let them decide for themselves whilst I make myself busy. Usually they will get their colours out, or puzzles, or simply start doing cartwheels and play gymnastics.

This moment allowed them to think for themselves; I didn't need to give constant suggestions and then get frustrated if they didn't like any. It is key to know that when the suggestion comes from themselves, they are more likely to spend longer doing it.

Getting involved

When they have spent some time doing whatever they chose, be mindful and join in with their activity. This will validate them and allow them to feel that finding their own entertainment is always a good idea. You don't obviously have to start doing cartwheels, but you can pretend to watch their gymnastics show, etc. If they are drawing and creating, why don't you join them? When's the last time you did that? It's not about not being good at it, it's about being a part of what they are doing and having fun with it. One time I recall my daughters and I sat and drew portraits of each other; it was so much fun, and yes, I was rubbish, but the memory that we created was anything but.

Are you OK?

Check in with yourself; how you feel and react will affect how children will feel and react. Mirror neurons in our brain mean we begin to mimic characteristics from other people if we are around them long enough. No doubt kids can test your patience, but have your go-to kit ready before the yelling and anger may arise. Whether it's letting them know you are having a time-out for a minute, putting some music on or getting a cup of tea. Show them some go-to tools too, tell them to draw a picture of what they are feeling, write down their thoughts or simply visualise what they would like to happen.

Breath work

Deep breathing is key here, taking breaths into your stomach for the count of three to five and then releasing it for three to five counts. This is a fantastic way to calm your mind and body down, and if your children are willing, then I actually do it with them. We sit together and practise 'magic breathing' or if they are really hysterical, I give them a hug and we press our stomachs together and start deep breathing. I turn it into a game and say, "Let's see whose belly goes out the furthest when we breathe in." Ninety-nine per cent of the time this always induces calmness.

Stay present and in tune

Stay mindful that they have been used to structure and routine for many weeks, and even though school holidays are awesome, it can feel a bit overwhelming at times when you don't always know what to do. You may have things planned, but also take time to find out if there's anything they would like to do; the answers may surprise you.

Stay present in all you do; this is an opportunity to really enjoy your home and space. You go through your home daily without really thinking about it, but this is a time to appreciate and value what you have. You have turned a house into a home, rooms filled with memories and mementoes; take a moment to look at the photos, the latest snack the kids are into or the clothes they have chosen to wear today. Take a minute, take a second to enjoy that; the more you enjoy the now, the less pressure you will feel to fill the next minute.

Nourish

Oatsome Flapjacks

This has definitely got to be my grab-and-go-to snack, and one of my favourites is bite-size flapjacks. These are super filling and very indulgent; plus, they will keep you going for a while.

Recipe

Ingredients

- 3 cups rolled oats
- 1 cup coconut oil or coconut butter
- ½ cup agave or maple syrup
- ¾ cup chopped cashews
- ¾ cup chopped dates

Method

1. Mix the oats with cashews and dates.
2. Add coconut oil and sweetener.
3. Thoroughly mix and then press into a small baking tray, keeping it about one inch thick.
4. Bake for thirty to forty minutes until golden.
5. Allow to cool and then cut into small pieces.

Yoga Pose

Downward Facing Dog

This pose is great in balancing the mind and body by stretching and strengthening the body, something definitely needed during half term.

Direction

1. Begin in a downward dog position, by coming on all fours and then as you breath in lift your hips up and knees off the floor.
2. Bring your heels towards the floor and let your head hang looking down.

Benefit

- This helps to calm the brain and relieve stress.
- It strengthens the arms and legs and really helps energise the body.

ELEVEN

School Holiday Mum Part 2

School's Out and Kids Are In

So it's that time of year again that we all hold our breath in anticipation for… the school holidays. It's taken the last eleven months (since the last school holidays) to carefully plan the six weeks of holiday. It's taken many meetings with the team – usually consisting of the parents, grandparents, uncles, aunties, other bribed and paid child-sitters – to figure out the geography and dates of where the child/ren will be going and when.

Then there's factoring in the fun family day trips and any other trips away: where to go, is it going to be entertaining enough, are there plentiful coffee shops en route and at destination, do we invite friends or will that reveal exactly how crazy my family is?

If we invite grandparents, then they have seen crazy many times over, in fact to the point where they feel sorry for me and are taking my children away from me (although secretly I think they take them because they think I am the crazy one, so maybe they are taking the children away for their safety). However, if we invite friends, then that means I have to be on my best behaviour and actually try to be extra patient and nice to the kids all day. It's always a dilemma whether to invite anyone on days out.

When the holidays descend upon us, we take the first few days in our stride. In fact, to our surprise, we actually enjoy it: no crazy chaotic morning, no running around looking for homework or throwing together a packed lunch; we settle into a false sense of security of, "Actually, I can do this!" Then it happens, everything in the house is eaten and played with, the restricted TV and gadget time slowly begins to increase, you can't bear the thought of hearing, "Muuuuummmmm," one more time, the careful scheduling and planning slowly begins to unravel.

The hours and days seem longer than ever (yes, it's summer, but it feels like summer in Russia); the kids aren't worn out enough so they go to bed late, but for some unknown reason (more research really needs to be invested in this), they still wake up early.

Even the fun-packed day trips are exhausting: preparing the backpack, packing all the just-in-case essentials, finding a parking space, fighting through the crowds, recovering from the shock at the cost of the food (why didn't I wake up earlier and bring a packed lunch?!) and remembering to actually smile for the camera. It's always a proud moment when returning from said trip having survived it knowing the kids can no longer say you don't take them anywhere.

Yes, there are definite great moments too: the moments when they are smiling, the moments they are entertained in the garden and you can enjoy a glass of something cold, the moments when they actually do listen, the moments they do give the occasional thank you, and everything in between.

School holidays are very definitely about high-fiving the perfect moments and embracing the imperfect moments.

It's OK when things aren't OK

Term time is very much about routine and structure – clubs, homework, tests, PE, etc. – all on certain days. The holidays definitely are the time to really enjoy and embrace the break from routine. Take a moment to really have fun with the unpredictable days, accept in advance that things won't always go to plan, but take away the pressure of needing it to be. This is great for kids to learn too, that it's OK if something doesn't work out because there is always plan B, C or D.

Plan B

Be mindful in being flexible and adaptable – if it's pouring with rain on a day when you had planned a trip or someone is poorly and plans have to be put on hold, allow the disappointment to enter but, just as easily, let it leave and replace it with creative excitement. You have a blank sheet to come up with something new; you couldn't control the situation, but you can absolutely control how you react to it. It doesn't matter what your age, you should have creative fun; you can get baking and make some cookies, or get some colours out and have a drawing competition, or go old school and play games like charades or cards.

Take your time

Take a moment to really enjoy the time with the kids without thinking of the to-do list; often the days we are at home we are constantly trying to get the chores done and we end up saying, "Wait one minute," far too many times. Often we are rushing the kids too when all they are doing is actually being present in the moment, usually at mealtimes or getting ready we will end up saying, "Hurry up," a million times. This is understandable on a time-restricted day, but if it's not and you are simply trying to load the dishwasher or move on to the next task, take a moment to let it be. Let them enjoy a few extra moments and let yourself be part of the moments too, take a little longer yourself when eating meals, take the time to enjoy a game, take the time to talk to them. When thoughts of the to-do list begin to appear, just observe them and let them go and focus back on the moment. Practise giving one hundred per cent in quality time.

You have my time and attention

I used to be really quick at wishing the time away – when my child would be reading a story and really looking at the pictures or stopping every now and then to absorb what she had read, I would tell her to hurry up… because in my mind I had jobs I needed to get on with. Now if thoughts like that enter my mind, I shut them down very quickly; my child is being much more mindful than me and really absorbing herself in the book, and that's such a joy to see. When they are really engrossed in telling me something and after a few minutes my mind wanders back to the time, again I shut it down and focus back on her, taking the time to really listen. They are living the moment of their story and being fully present with their thoughts and feelings; I need to continue to practise doing the same.

Mindfulness on the hour every hour

Every five minutes of every hour of the day you are with your child/ren in the holidays. If it's practical (for example, not appropriate when you are midway on a rollercoaster), stop and practise being mindful. Experience everything through your senses in that moment: what can you see, hear, smell, taste and feel. Whatever the scenario is, just enjoy the moment, whether it is calm or chaos.

You are Amazing
You are Brave
You are Strong
You are Enough
You are Perfectly Imperfect

Nourish

Chocolate Chip Cookies... Let's Get Baking

Something to do on your own or together with your child/ren. There may be mess and spillage and more washing and tidying to do, but that just shows how much creative fun you have had. The aroma that will come from the oven will be enough to make you forget the to-do list. Beware, these are very MORE-ish.

Recipe

Ingredients

- 2 cup spelt flour or whole-wheat flour
- ½ cup ground almonds
- 1 teaspoon baking powder
- 1 teaspoon baking soda
- ½ cup coconut sugar
- ½ cup coconut oil melted
- ¼ cup almond milk
- Chocolate chips
- Pinch of pink salt

Method

1. In a mixing bowl, add the flour, almonds, baking powder and baking soda, and mix.
2. Add the coconut sugar and mix.
3. Add the milk, pink salt and coconut oil.
4. Add the chocolate chips.
5. Form nice dough and then put in the fridge to chill for twenty minutes.
6. Once chilled, take a tablespoon of the dough and roll into a ball, then gently flatten. Continue to do this and place onto a baking sheet.
7. Bake for thirty minutes or until just golden at 180 degrees.

Yoga Pose and Movement

Shavasana

This is the perfect pose to practise daily, which is the resting pose, a total surrender of the body and mind.

Direction

1. Simply lie down with your arms and legs uncrossed and palms facing upwards.
2. Take gentle breaths in and out, focusing only on the breath.
3. Allow all the parts of the body to surrender and relax.
4. When any distracting thoughts appear, simply observe but do not pay attention, then focus back on your breath.
5. Lie for five to ten minutes.

Benefits

- Complete physical and mental relaxation.

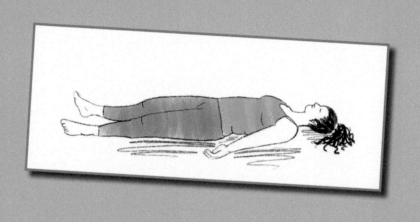

TWELVE

School Mum

W ow! OK, so the school mum is just being a mum on a whole different level, right? I actually think they should invent a calendar just for the school mum – you have those family planners and meal planners, but they really need one just for schools... maybe bespoke for my school... which automatically updates with dates of things that are going on... hmmmmm (because emails and newsletters and bits of paper just aren't doing the job). Sorry, went off on a tangent there.

My nerves actually start going at the end of August, because just as much as I know the kids are due back at school very soon, it also means my diary is going to look multi-coloured once more. As with most kids, my girls go to various after-school clubs and just managing to get to these on the right day is a bonus. However, when the letters and updates start coming that it's Victorian dress-up day, bring in a cake day, homework due in on a Monday, spellings in on a Friday, class assembly on this date, summer fete on that date, optional maths challenge, bring a parent to read on a Wednesday morning, etc., etc., it can feel a bit like *whoooaaaaa*.

No matter how many ways I try to remember from sticking letters on my fridge, putting it in the diary, thinking I have plenty of days for said task, the time just flies, and the next minute some mum will announce on the private WhatsApp group, "Do they need a snack for tomorrow's school trip?" And as I read it, panic sets in, my mind speaks: *School trip, what school trip? I thought that was ages away. Yes, Sheena, it was ages away when you remembered four weeks ago but now it's tomorrow.* Off I go, quick run around the kitchen or last-minute dash to Tesco to see what I can put together. (PS, how does that WhatsApp mum seem to remember EVERYTHING? The one who knows every detail about everything, the cool, calm one, without a trace of a stress line.)

It's not just the super-busy school diary, it's everything else that's attached to it too: the school runs and fighting for a parking space, walking into the school gates and wondering if anyone will smile back at you or even talk to you, or if you go at pick-up time in your jogging bottoms, are you going to get judged? If you don't bake a cake or volunteer, are the PTA going to put you on their secret blacklist?!

Then there's the awful thought of when you compare your child to others, and even worse is when you start wondering if other parents start judging your child. Why's my child not being picked for the main part... again... or will my child ever move up to the reading levels all those other kids have, or my child doesn't seem very sporty... or arty... or anything, and the worst one is when you think your child doesn't seem to have any friends... gosh, that one usually breaks my heart.

So many emotions can run through us every single day, all related to just being the school mum. Sometimes you even question whether you are up to the role of school mum. It takes a lot of love, patience and kindness to ourselves for getting through each school week... yes, OK, and coffee and cake too.

Mindfulness and Motivation Tips

You are one in a billion

Take a moment to realise that there is no other mum in the world like you, and that's what makes you so incredible, wonderful and unique. Whatever stresses or pressures you may be feeling in this very moment, just let them float away, just for this minute, just for now, even. Any thoughts that are causing the stress, put them in a little cloud and let them simply float away. Replace them with loving, kind thoughts towards yourself, reminding yourself that your children absolutely adore you for everything you do. You show up for them every single day, giving them the comfort and confidence to grow. You are their cheerleader every moment, and they feel so much love and security in knowing that. They don't care about what you wear, or if you still can't park properly, or even if you can't bake a cake (they care more about if you buy them the cake at the cake sale); they simply care that you are there.

Practise what you preach

We tell our children it doesn't matter what place or score they come in tests, sports day or performances; we tell them to simply try their best and have fun. So why do we not give ourselves that same advice? Why do we put so much pressure on being perfect and getting it right each and every time? When it was all getting too much for me, I made a conscious decision to simply not sweat the small stuff anymore. I would still put the effort in and try my best, but if things didn't always go to plan then I would move on. If I forgot to hand in a reply slip for something, or forgot a packed lunch one day, I accepted that errors can happen and I would try again.

Popcorn

It is easy to fall in the trap of comparing your child to others, but remember all children are like popcorn kernels – they will all pop, but some just earlier or later than others. As long as your child is walking out of the school gate with a semi-smile then that's all that matters, anything else is just work in progress. They are growing and adapting to learning and play, but also learning new things every single day. Everyone's journey is unique; your child doesn't need to be great at anything or everything to still be great.

They won't always be dressed up as a donkey

See everything as an opportunity; when your child comes home with a letter, they usually have some enthusiasm for whatever it is, even some excitement. Our reaction may not always mirror this, but choose to have some fun with it. Instead of seeing it as a thing to do, really be present with it and take a moment to enjoy it. Enjoy seeing how they look when they dress up (come on, it's only a handful of times you will see them dressed up as a sheep or a donkey, and they'll make great pics for the eighteenth birthday party), enjoy the class assembly; whatever it is, practise being mindful when you are there by focusing your attention on the moment and letting go of any thoughts based on time and your to-do list.

Friendships

The times when your child may come home telling you they have no friends, that no one wants to play with them or that they've had a falling-out can be really upsetting. This used to really upset me. I would worry about them and wish I could be at school to comfort and protect them. The thought of them wandering around on their own watching others play would be heart-breaking.

However, I soon learnt that I had to let them go through that; it was part of life and part of growing. Yes, I could teach them to be strong and give them options on what to do if they didn't have friends to go to that day, but they also needed time and space to figure things out too.

It would teach them to communicate, to listen, to maybe learn how to make different friends, to understand things don't always go to plan, that this can happen at any age.

Have fun

Have fun with the journey; don't put yourself under pressure because it will serve you no purpose. Enjoy each day for what it is, enjoy the moments. Often we are always wishing for the next phase, from sleepless nights to weaning, from walking to going to school, from school to teenagers, etc. Instead of wishing the years away when certain times are a little tough (and I have been guilty of this), take the time to find joy in the day. How cute they look in the school uniform, the seconds it takes for them to ask what's for dinner, the excitement of a school trip they have been told about, the fun they had with a friend.

Nourish

Flip-ing Scrummy Pancakes

These are great for morning, lunch, brunch or anytime. You can add various toppings, including grated apple, berries, chopped bananas, nuts, date syrup and much more. I love pancakes; my favourite time for these is on a lazy Sunday morning.

Recipe

Ingredients
Dry

- 2 cups spelt flour (buckwheat for gluten-free)
- 2 teaspoons baking powder
- 2 tablespoons coconut sugar
- Sprinkle of salt

Wet

- 2 cups almond milk (or milk of choice)
- 2 tablespoons apple cider

Method

1. Mix the dry ingredients together and add together with the pre-mixed wet ingredients. Keep whisking so the mixture is nice and bubbly.
2. Take a ladle of the mixture and fry in a small pan using coconut oil or butter; let it cook on each side for a few minutes.
3. Add toppings of choice.

Yoga Pose

Dancer's Pose

A great pose that helps open the heart and solar plexus, giving you a good connection with your own personal power whilst improving your balance and concentration. Connection from within is vital in strengthening your mind when feeling 'school mum' thoughts.

Direction

1. Stand with your feet together, shift your weight to the left foot.
2. Bend the right knee and bring the right heel towards the right glute; with your right hand, take hold of the inside arch of the right foot.
3. Stay grounded with the left foot.
4. Lift your chest as you slowly extend the right foot back, keeping your hips square.
5. As you look up, stretch your left hand forwards.
6. Focus on a spot to keep steady for a few breaths.
7. To end, gently release your grip on the foot and return to standing.
8. Repeat on the other side.

Benefits

- This beautiful posture gives courage, love and compassion by opening up the solar plexus.
- It also strengthens the hip flexors and leg muscles.

THIRTEEN

Stressed Mum

————

I t's one of those days or weeks where everything has gotten on top of you. Maybe it's the full moon, maybe one too many things aren't going to plan, you've possibly stretched yourself thin and are at breaking point. We can all experience times like this, where it's been a busy period with life events, school events, family events, etc., and you just want time to stop for a few hours whilst you pause and take a long breath.

It can be really easy to constantly keep on going, to keep running around and holding things together without stopping for any self-care. It then gets to a point where you feel run down, low on energy and mood, and need time to recharge. This is not a sign that you aren't capable or not in control or that you aren't doing a good job. This is also definitely not a sign that you aren't cut out for parenthood or that you can't cope. When we are feeling a little stressed or low, our negative self-dialogue decides to show up and can make us spiral into not feeling good about ourselves.

As mentioned, this can happen to each and every one of us; we can be sat on the sofa and reflecting how we ended up here feeling like this. We will wonder if we can get back to a state of happiness again. We may wonder if there even is a place of happiness in this hectic life because it seems to be in the distance.

What is important here is to remember how vital self-care is; we are constantly serving other people around us, from the kids, family, colleagues and friends – and in between that, making sure the house stays standing – that we neglect to serve ourselves. Once again, we come last in the queue when we need the love and care the most, without stopping to check in with yourself more often you will not be able to be present for others.

Mindfulness and Motivation Tips

Mindful body

Once a week simply ask yourself, **Are you OK?** Really take that time to tune in with yourself. What emotional thoughts are coming through; are there any associated physical symptoms, such as headaches or muscle tension? This is a good opportunity to sit on the floor cross-legged, palm gently on your lap and back nice and straight (if this is not comfortable, take a seat in whichever position is comfortable to you), slowly close your eyes and take a few minutes to inhale and exhale deeply. Acknowledge your thoughts for a couple of minutes, and then slowly start putting them in imaginary clouds and let them float away. As each cloud floats away, focus on your breathing, and when another thought arrives, let that one float away too. If you notice any areas in your body feeling tense, try and breathe into that area too.

Mindful start and end

Always ensure that you start and end your day in a positive way; it's very easy to begin the day with chaos. Maybe start the day with a positive intention, quote or affirmation, or practise your breath work for one minute to instil the calmness. When you end your day, have half an hour of unwinding, whether that's having a bath, reading a book, listening to music or meditation, or maybe even writing in a journal.

Time out

Ensure you take time out, even if it's just ten minutes in the day, to simply stop. When we are on the go from morning to night it can get too much, so make sure you find that time to stop. In fact, as I write this, just prior to me getting back to the typing I had to take ten minutes. It was Sunday but still a busy day. I was trying to be present and play with the kids to spend time with them, then there were the various meals that had to be made and the house that needed tidying up; I also had to find time to fit in a bit of work, all whilst been called upon every few minutes. So once they had gone to sleep and before I carried on to the next task I took ten minutes out and listened to a motivational podcast which helped me to realign myself again.

Smile

Give yourself a smile and a hug; tell yourself that this is just a blip and that this time will pass. You have had many moments like this before and it is just your body and mind's way of telling you to slow down and give yourself some attention. Listen and read the signs of yourself and do something that makes you feel good. Serve yourself before serving others.

Nourish

Snickers – Style Smoothie

I love this indulgent drink which doesn't take long to make, it's full of yummy ingredients and really does take like a chocolatey milkshake.

Recipe

Ingredients
- 1 glass nut milk
- 1 small banana
- 1 heaped tablespoon peanut butter
- 1 tablespoon cacao powder
- 1 teaspoon maca powder (a great adaptogen in healing natural stressors within the body)

Method
1. Place everything in a blender, whizz and serve chilled.

Yoga Pose

Easy Pose

Anything easy at a moment like this sounds good to me.

Direction

1. Gently find a spot on the floor, sit cross-legged and put your hands in prayer pose.
2. Stay like this for a few minutes, focusing on your inhale and exhale of breath.

Benefits

- It is a nice hip-opener but can also reduce anxiety and instil inner calm.

FOURTEEN

Going on Holiday Mum

Woohoo, the holiday is booked, and you are super excited to be flying off for a week in the sun. You ask people if they have any holidays planned this year simply as an opportunity to be able to say, "Yes, I am going abroad," when they ask the question back.

You buy some new holiday clothes, get yourself waxed, manicured and pedicured, and then you attempt to pack the suitcase. Now, in my case, there's three girls in the family (including me), and my husband fails to understand what this means... every time. We need various types of footwear: plane ones, beach ones, evening ones and just-in-case ones. We also need clothes to accompany all of the said footwear; we then need various clips, grips, hairbands and the odd bracelet or two. Then I have to figure out how to tell my husband (again) that he can only bring two pairs of clothes because there is no more room.

I am feeling smug that everything is under control and we are ready to go; this is how you may feel too. Now you have barely started the car journey to the airport and you will most likely hear, "Are we there yet?" You tell them no, but you are prepared for this; you have packed entertainment and a snack… twenty minutes later it's all eaten and they are bored. You resort to eye-spy and counting coloured cars. You even start singing nursery rhymes for some bizarre reason. (No? Just me, then.)

The plane ride is fine (just about) and then you reach your holiday destination – hallelujah. You check in and head to your room. You get yourselves changed and head to the pool; you think you are finally about to relax… well, think again… you hear the famous words – "Muuuuummmmm" – over and over again. "Where's my goggles?", "I need the toilet" (again), "Mum, I'm hungry" (ten minutes after lunch), "Mum, I can't find my ball", "Mum, that other kid splashed me", "Mum, can you play with me?", etc.

At mealtimes, if it is an all-inclusive-type place, you will feel like you are up and down like a yoyo, getting your meals, getting their meals, getting your dessert, helping choose their dessert, getting your sides, whilst helping carry their plates. You tell yourself you earnt that fifth dessert just for all the walking you just did – you are positive that it hit the steps requirement for the day.

If it's self-catering, then for the kids every single thing will taste different and they won't want to eat. You can forget about the cheese or yoghurts.

Your bedroom looks like a jumble sale with clothes flung left right and centre, and you actually have to attempt to find your bed underneath it all.

Sometimes kids like the kids' clubs and others don't; either way you feel guilty for sending them there. You want to spend time with them, but you want time for yourself. You're happy you are away, but it's actually becoming a little exhausting too. You're trying to enjoy yourself and some moments you actually do, usually when your child is right next to you and you are not constantly looking for them to make sure they aren't being kidnapped.

You want to be having the time of your life, but sometimes it's not always so simple or easy to.

Mindfulness and Motivation Tips

Mindful Scenes

This is a great opportunity to practise mindful senses. You are in a new place, so everything is going to take time to adapt to. Take a moment to really see the colours, hear the sounds, and feel everything around you. Don't worry that you are hearing 'Mum' one too many times; take a moment or two just for you. Do this when you are by the pool, in the room and going for meals. This may not always be easy, but keep practising it at every opportunity you get throughout the day. This will keep you focused on the moment and will enable you to appreciate the present time.

Making the Unfamiliar Familiar

Acknowledge that it is all new and unfamiliar to the kids too – the food, place and surroundings – so they are looking for comfort in you. Yes, it's exciting and there's lots of fun to be had, but sometimes with that a little fear can creep in, and thoughts of, *What if I get lost?*, *What if my mum can't find me?*, *What if my mum forgets where I am?*, etc. It's being mindful that these worries can be in the kid's mind.

Early Bird

If it's possible, maybe wake up a little earlier and take a day to grab breakfast by yourself or go for a coffee on your own in the afternoon, or even a little stroll. A little time for yourself, letting your kids know in advance that this is what you will be doing.

Gentle Rules

Set some light rules, let your kids know that if they can have a swim for twenty minutes without calling you, you will then go in and play with them. A little compromise and meeting them halfway. If they fold their clothes away at the end of the day, then maybe there might be time to play a game together. Explaining that the more time they can create for you, the more time they can actually have with you.

It's all Okay

Rest, nourish and absorb as much vitamin D as you can, and know that all holidays can be perfectly imperfect. Enjoy the new things the kids are seeing, eating and doing. Enjoy the perfectly imperfect memories you are creating.

Nourish

Fruit Bowl – Fruity Fun When on Holiday

This is my absolute favourite thing to have on holiday. I love exploring their seasonal fruit, choosing a variety and chopping it up in my bowl. This can be done, whether you are being catered for or if it's self-catering. I then love to add any nuts and seeds that are available. This is a yummy, colourful, vibrant bowl, bursting with juices and being complemented with the crunchy nuts.

Option: if they have a whole fruit like papaya, scoop out the seeds, replace that with yoghurt, nuts and seeds, and then eat spoons of the fruit with what you have just topped it with.

Yoga Pose

Dolphin Pose

Nothing like being abroad and doing a dolphin pose; this pose is known to relieve headaches and fatigue too, something which you may encounter on the trip.

Direction

1. Come onto the floor on your hands and knees, keep your forearms down, elbows under the shoulders and hands clasped together.
2. Curl your toes under and then, as you exhale, lift your knees away from the floor and bottom up.
3. Keep pressing your forearms into the floor; you can straighten your knees or leave them bent depending on how you feel.
4. Stay in that position for thirty seconds.

Benefits

- This pose provides relief from headaches, insomnia and fatigue.
- It also strengthens the upper body, arms and legs.

FIFTEEN

Happy Mum

Today you are in a great mood; you don't even know why. You haven't won the lottery, it's not your birthday and the kids haven't given you a lie in. However, you feel good. You put the music on and start singing and dancing around the kitchen, you tidy up after the kids without saying a word, you even tell them you'll be making their favourite dinner tonight. Your children think you are either ill or something scary is about to come their way.

Today you simply don't have a care in the world; you feel free and you love it. You have messy hair but you don't care; you have make-up on but you feel your beauty from within; you're in your joggers and are happy to be the school mum giving your kid a big squeeze; you're in your corporate wear but you feel all the power from within your heart.

You feel happy because you get to be a mum. A mum in a messy house and clean house, a mum when you are driving from one place to another to chilling on the sofa, a mum where you are making meals and looking at homework and everything in between. Through it all, you feel a sense of freedom because none of the 'stuff' matters, none of the chaos matters, none of the squabbles matter, none of the ever-changing weeks matter, because the one constant that remains the same is you get to be a loved, perfectly imperfect mum. Nothing will ever change or replace that, and that feeling alone is priceless and worth a thousand children-shaped hugs and kisses.

Mindfulness and Motivation Tips

Self-Love
I'll say this all day and every day, be kind to you and don't put pressure on anything. Embrace the day, be as mindful as you can and enjoy each hour as it unfolds.

Right Intention

Have no expectations for anything (don't expect to do your hair in the morning, so when you do, it's a bonus), put the effort in and have the intention, but don't be consumed by the outcome.

Energy
Every day, turn the music up and have a dance (even when you really don't feel like it). It will lift you up and make you smile, guaranteed.

Smile
Keep smiling – smiling is infectious and you will spread and receive the positivity.

Show Up
Simply being there for yourself and your children is all that matters.

Time Out

Let today be the day where you stop for 30 minutes and really interact or get creative with the kids, dance with them, play a game of cards or get the art set and just have fun.

Nourish

Virgin Mojito

Say cheers with this refreshing virgin mojito. With all that energy and happy dancing, this is the perfect way to cool down, and if you love a little sparkle in your day then this is the drink for you.

Recipe

Ingredients
- Sparkling water
- 1 teaspoon agave
- 1 fresh lemon or lime squeezed
- Mint leaves

Method
1. In a glass, add chilled sparkling water, the spoon of agave, a squeeze of one lime and a few mint leaves.
2. Leave to sit for a few minutes and then enjoy.

Yoga Pose

Happy Baby Pose

Nothing quite so freeing and liberating than the happy baby pose. This is exactly what a baby does when they haven't a worry in the world.

Direction

1. Lie on your back.
2. As you exhale, bend your knees and grip the outside of your feet with your hands, or grip your big toe, or hold the inside of your feet on the ball of the foot
3. If this is difficult, you can use a belt looped over each foot.
4. Ankles should be directly over the knees; you can then gently rock your body side to side. (Keep your tailbone on the floor.)

Benefits

- As well as stretching the spine, this calms the brain and relieves stress.
- It also regulates the flow of nutrients in the body, promoting inner wellness.
- The pose also activates a positive energy by changing the ever-busy mind into one of a carefree child; it invigorates the mind and reduces anxiety.

Affirmations

Start of Day

I always start my day and end my day as positively as possible. I appreciate sometimes this can be tricky; however, I do believe it is possible, especially if you only require a minimum of five minutes (longer if you can). Time isn't lost, so we don't have to find it. However, we can utilise it better and make space for self-care… after all, I am sure we all sneak in a couple of minutes here and there to check Facebook, Insta or emails.

I start my day with a few deep breaths and saying positive affirmations. Affirmations are a great way to feel present, feel good and begin the day with good intentions.

Positive affirmations are positive statements, ideally said in the present tense to help overcome negative thoughts and emotions, and help make positive changes. Positive thoughts can transform your behaviour and your outlook in life. Practising affirmations will allow you to be more conscious of your thoughts in the day, you will be more mindful of any negative dialogue creeping in and can then change this to positive dialogue. You may be having a bad day and tell yourself, *I am having a bad day, everything is going wrong*, and be consumed in this thought all day, or you can be mindful and say, *I have had some setbacks today – however, I can learn and adapt and move forward and be open to better things that can come my way.*

When you wake up in the morning, take ten deep breaths, choose an affirmation from below or make one up that you resonate with. Say it in your mind three times, then say it out loud three times, really meaning it.

Affirmations:

- I am calm.
- I am peaceful.
- I am kind.
- I am patient.
- I am ambitious.
- I am creating change.
- I am nourishing my body.
- I am letting go of everything that no longer serves me.
- I believe in myself.
- I am free of worry.
- I am proud of myself.
- I am becoming confidant.
- I am stronger today than yesterday.
- I am worthy.
- I am right where I need to be.
- I am an awesome mum.
- I am beautiful, smart and living life.

My favourite one:

- I AM ENOUGH.

Gratitude Journal

always end my day with thoughts of gratitude. It's so easy to be caught up in the whirlwind of a day and think about it being busy, tiring, hectic, full-on, etc., but these thoughts will make you feel those words even more and you can easily lose sight of anything good that may have happened.

Taking a moment to really think about the 'what made me smile' moments can really start changing the way you see each day. Initially you may even have to really think about the good things, but with daily practice you will really naturally begin to notice more of the good parts of the day and less of the negative bits, and the negative parts will stop having the huge impact they once did.

This is an activity I also like doing with the kids as well as on my own.

Instead of the conversation with my kids, which used to go:

Mum: How was your day, kids?
Kids: Fine/good.
Mum: What did you do?
Kids: Nothing/can't remember.

I now ask them:

Mum: What were three good things that happened today?

It's such a great conversation; we can all share our views on the day and it reminds them of what went well too.

You can also keep a journal and note down three things you were grateful for and why you were grateful for them. This is a great way to end the night; it reduces stress and anxiety and allows for a good rest and peace of mind.

Gratitude Practice

- Keep a gratitude jar: Have a jar with some cut-up paper ready on the side. Every time you or someone in the family feels grateful for something, write it down and pop it in the jar. Every six to twelve months, take them out and read it out loud together. It's lovely to remember the moments of gratitude throughout the year.
- Gratitude tree: Another option is to draw a large tree with just branches, you can then write what you are grateful for on cut-out leaves or that you can stick on or draw leaves on. The tree can get bigger and bigger with all the leaves of gratitude.
- Letters: Take time to each write a letter of gratitude to someone; it could be to a family member, friend, teacher — anyone at all.

- Talking: Tell someone you were grateful for an action they may have done that made you happy or meant a lot to you. A simple thank you and a smile can go a long way.
- Sharing: Spread the positivity by smiling and asking how someone is, even if you wouldn't usually talk to them. Giving someone the time of day could mean a lot and something they would be grateful for.
- Mindful: Be mindful of the small moments you feel grateful for: the cuddle from your child, the excitement when you make their favourite food, the words they read at bedtime to you, their need for you, etc.

Meditation

This meditation is great at any time of the day, or just before going to sleep, and is suitable for all ages. Often our emotions and thoughts can cause physical reactions in the body. Sometimes these are noticeable, other times they build up and begin causing long-term pain. This can include headaches, muscle tension, neckache, stomach cramps and nausea. It's always good to check in with our bodies.

Find a comfortable space to lie down, either on the bed or on a mat.

Lie down on your back with your arms to the side and palms facing upwards, your legs stretched out and uncrossed.

Gently close your eyes and focus on simply being here and lying down. Any distracting thoughts that come into the mind (such as the to-do list), simply observe the thought and let it go, focusing back on the here and now. Focus how your whole body is feeling supported by the bed or floor, how the clothes are feeling against your skin, and simply listen to any sounds you may hear, allowing your body to relax nice and deeply.

Take nice deep breaths in and out.

Bring your attention to your toes, feet and legs; allow all the muscles to really let go and relax. Allow the legs to sink even further on the floor. Visualise in your mind each and every nerve of the muscles softening and relaxing.

Gently move your focus to your spine and back; as you inhale, breathe right into the spine. Allow any tension in the lower and upper back to melt away, visualise and feel the muscles relaxing and becoming heavier and connecting deeper to the support it's lying on.

Bring your awareness to the fingertips and hands; allow them to really flop and become loose. Allow the muscles in the arms and shoulders to gently relax; bring awareness so that your shoulders are being gently pulled down, releasing it of any tension.

Bring your awareness towards your stomach area, breathe nice deep breaths into the stomach allowing your body to feel even calmer and more relaxed. Moving towards your heart centre, really feel it lifting with each beat, filling and expanding with love.

Gently move your awareness to your neck area, visualise all the nerves around it relaxing. As your neck relaxes, think about the passageway opening up even more to allow those deep breaths to pass through.

Bring your awareness to your face and allow all the muscles around your features to soften, allow the lids to become a little heavier, relax the jaw and cheeks, soften the tongue and ensure there is a little space between the two rows of teeth.

Allow your head to feel relaxed and supported, and allow any thoughts to sit in little clouds and float away as you refocus on your breath and the here and now.

Take a moment to really feel your body, feel it relaxing, feel it being nourished and looked after with love and kindness. Take a few breaths with this feeling.

If you do this before you go to sleep, you can end here and continue to sleep.

Otherwise, slowly start to bring movement to your feet and fingers by giving them a wiggle, then gently turn to a side and slowly sit up. Take a couple of breaths before opening your eyes.

Well done.

To-Be List

We are always making to-do lists, and a favourite thing of mine to do is to tick one thing off the list and add three more things. Well, an equally, if not more important, list is the to-*be* list, and here the list should look like something this (in no particular order):

To be:

- Happy.
- Confident.
- Relaxed.
- Rested.
- Nourished.
- Energised.
- Calm.
- Positive.
- Creative.
- Fun.

- Feel enough.
- Loved.

To achieve some of these things, here are a few suggestions:

- Take up movement, either dancing around the living room, doing a YouTube workout, going to the gym, going for a walk or taking up a class.
- Connect with others, whether that's friends, colleagues or family. Pick up the phone for a chat, meet for a coffee, go out for dinner, have a movie night in or organise a fun activity.
- Take up some form of art and craft. It's not about being talented, it's about having fun and letting your creative side flow. I went on a recent arty party where eight total novices learnt and had a go at painting for a few hours; it really was so much fun. It wasn't about the end result being perfect, it was simply to let go, enjoy and connect with something new.
- Be with nature. Whatever the weather, go for a walk, enjoy the seasons, the colours, smells, sounds and feel free in the beautiful space around you. Grab a coffee, or a book, or simply be with your thoughts. Have no agenda but to simply enjoy being out there.
- Give yourself some attention by running a hot bath, lighting candles, reading a book, listening to music or having a little nap. Do what makes you feel good and loved. Schedule it in on a regular basis and really enjoy that time.
- Nourish yourself with colourful, vibrant, healthy food. The right foods can really uplift you and make you feel energised. Try a new cookbook for inspiration or even some of the recipes in here. I would love to hear about what you have created.

Perfectly Imperfect Mum

can genuinely say that having put into practice every single one of the tips in this book in my daily life, I feel such a sense of inner peace and inner calm. I used to be consumed with anxiety, overwhelmed with motherhood and constantly fearful of messing things up or things going wrong.

My patience used to be at an all-time low because of my emotions; my husband would simply be asking how my day was and that would turn me into some sort of psycho.

The minute I thought I had things under control, a new challenge would be thrown my way. I had a rollercoaster of emotions during my rollercoaster days. I didn't know who to turn to and where to go. Even though my husband is incredible, I was the one who had to deal with how I was feeling. He or anyone else couldn't change that; it was only something I could do.

Studying, learning and implementing all the techniques has absolutely changed not just my life but my family life. I am able to respond rather than react, I am able to control my thoughts and emotions and not let them overwhelm me, and I am able to recover from setbacks much quicker than ever before, which is so vital in moving forward.

Embrace that not one thing in life is perfect, and that is what makes it interesting, unique and incredible. It enables us to learn, grown and develop, and can open us up to many unexpected opportunities.

Life as a mum will be filled with the most wonderful, crazy, beautiful and chaotic moments. Every day will be a learning day, every day something new or different will show up (including things like random facts about a gecko). Every day the unfamiliar will become familiar, and every day you will, whatever shows up in the day, YOU will also show up and take it on.

Every day remind yourself that YOU ARE THE MOST BEAUTIFUL AND INCREDIBLE ONE-IN-A-MILLION PERFECTLY IMPERFECT MUM and your child wouldn't want you any other way.